I0559651

FROM THE
EAGLE'S NEST
TO THE LION'S DEN

MIRKA ANDERSON

Copyright © 2025 by Mirka Anderson

Paperback: 978-1-966652-87-8
Hardcover: 978-1-967820-30-6
eBook: 978-1-966652-88-5
Library of Congress Control Number: 2025906450

All rights reserved. No part of this publication may be reproduced, distributed, or
transmitted in any form or by any electronic or mechanical means, without the prior
written permission of the publisher, except in the case of brief quotations embodied in
critical reviews and certain other noncommercial uses permitted by copyright law.

This Book is a work of nonfiction.

Ordering Information:

Prime Seven Media
518 Landmann St.
Tomah City, WI 54660

Printed in the United States of America

With love to
Caroline, Emma and Sophie xxx

ABOUT THE AUTHOR

The authoress is a linguist, a speech and language therapist, a mother of three and a documentary director, reminiscing over five decades of life-changing and character-forming events that she has experienced since leaving socialist Poland and arriving in capitalist England.

Mirka Kiersztejn was born in Warszawa, Poland in 1951. She graduated from the University of Warsaw with a diploma in linguistics (interpreting English and Spanish) in 1973. She left Poland for England around 50 years ago.

In 1975, Mirka got married and had her first child, Caroline, the following year. She received a diploma in speech therapy from City Lit College, London in 1981. The following year she left England for New Zealand and travelled via Sri Lanka, Indonesia, Thailand and Australia for one-and-a-half months.

During 1982-3, Mirka worked in Auckland hospitals as a speech therapist in neurological disorders and dementia clinics. She returned to England in 1983 via Tahiti, USA (four months' travel in a camper across the States) and Mexico. In 1984, her second daughter

Emma was born with Down Syndrome and a life-threatening heart condition and Mirka has been her carer for 40 years.

From 1986-2007, she worked as a communication therapist in a private psychiatric hospital. Mirka's third daughter Sophie was born in 1990.

Mirka received a MSc in human communication from the University of London in 1992.

In 2017 Mirka also acted as the director of the documentary "the sky is the limit" initiating her one-woman mission to change social perceptions and attitudes towards Down Syndrome people. She has received 50 awards to date, and counting, from the USA (Hawaii, California, New Mexico, New York), Mexico, Chile, Venezuela, Spain, Germany, Poland, Russia, India, Australia and Bhutan.

Mirka Anderson, nee Kiersztejn

ABOUT THE BOOK

"From the Eagle's Nest to the Lion's Den" is an incredibly evocative and unique autobiography and memoir, covering the author's journey from a country in sociopolitical turmoil to travelling the world. From the very beginning, the readers get an insight into what life was like in socialist Poland with the system controlling its people and the narratives through propaganda.

With her moving to the UK, we experience the author's world changing as she starts her journey of being exposed to new cultures, languages, traditions, people and religions. As the audience, we find ourselves completely engrossed as the author steps into her dreamland and finds freedom in London.

The author struggles in her pursuit of high-quality education from the universities in England, as she fights her way through all obstacles to fulfil her dreams.

This book is more than a simple mixture of adventure and biography. It also brings in the idea of a travelogue, which makes the central theme of the book far more interesting than one might believe it to be. With the great details of the landmarks and sites in England, from London to further afield, the audience gets to experience and visualise all these tourism spots that are filled with adventure and history.

As we continue to read the author's journey from her marriage and having her dearest children to her travelling the world with her family, we find ourselves getting lost in the life of a person who lives life to the fullest and allows herself to be exposed to different perspectives and outlooks on life.

It is enjoyable reading about her travels in various countries. On reading about all the visits, we found our favourite destinations to be Tunisia, Greece, and New Zealand. It was really interesting to see how the cultures of each country were so different, and yet somehow how they all were similar in terms of hospitality, history and landscapes.

One thing that was quite evident from reading this book was that, despite travelling the world and living abroad, Poland and her roots always remained very close to her heart. As the author herself says in the book: "And one can take a Pole out of Poland, but cannot take Poland out of a Pole."

Seeing the author write a Polish language course for English speakers and help the differently-abled through her mission and documentary, is really inspirational and gives a message that through compassion, unity and tolerance we can solve all our problems. And so, this book inspires the readers to take action and make plans for something adventurous. As the author nicely puts it: "Seize the day!"

CONTENTS

PREFACE

My cultural enrichment process started in London, and continued in Barcelona then back in London and then during a round-the-world voyage via Dubai, Sri Lanka, Indonesia and Australia with a one-year stopover in New Zealand. On the way back, the route included Tahiti, Moorea and Bora Bora and led to the USA, which became our home for four months, travelling its vast territory in our camper via Baja California, Mexico and across the States to New York.

Life-changing events were of a more personal nature; my marriage, the arrival of my first daughter Caroline - my Sweetie - then Emma - my Star who has Down syndrome, and the baby of the family Sophie - my Sunshine. That, together with my studies, writing the Polish language course for English speakers, supporting the differently-abled, and celebrating my mission to change social attitudes towards them via my documentary "The sky is the limit", are some of the influencing experiences and challenges of my journey. The documentary covers the life success of Emma, who despite social, physical, and psychological adversities, managed to surface as a prolific artist, recognised by an exhibition in the Tate Modern, London. The film has been submitted to multiple international film festivals, and so far, has been awarded 50 prizes from Hawaii to Bhutan. And it continues to be a world success...

I hope reading this western autobiography will bring back the essential meaning of our existence; seize the day and where there is a will, there is a way!

CHAPTER I
HELLO LONDON!

Warszawa, Poland

London, UK

I t is actually happening. I AM going to make my dream come true after graduating from Warsaw University with a diploma in modern languages (English and Spanish)!

After one year of preparations, which required patience and tolerance of the two diverse political systems at the height of the Cold War, I am on my way. In Poland, the red tape was very tight, and it took some thinking to enable my departure. The system was bent on total control and glorification of the leadership of the Polish United Workers Party, and the presumed, or rather enforced, people's admiration for its superior effectiveness in guiding its nation in the post-war recovery under the protectorate and the watchful eye of our Russian brothers over the eastern border.

The slogans were everywhere, telling us on a daily basis that we were with the party and its moves were in our national security interests. The visual and auditory propaganda was strong and often referred to the rotten system of capitalism, which focused on money-making and consumerism. The actual feeling of social equality was in every walk of life. From schools, where all participated in education without exception, until the age of 18, having to learn more than 12 subjects (including the obvious compulsory Russian language and military training), regardless of abilities in everyday life challenges.

There was a strong feeling of camaraderie as the times were tough and required a lot of system manipulation to survive. The supervision of citizens' whereabouts was of the essence as to not allow any contamination of peaceful socialism with invasive capitalism. Hence, the passports, if issued, would be pending the decision of the governmental bodies who employed pen pushers.

The Workers' Party members, no doubt, were guarded by the respectful special service units, and passports had to be applied for each time one wanted to travel abroad. They were valid for two years, and all tourism in the Socialist Bloc was allowed without obstacles, leading to the development of spectacular networking on the black market amongst the Bloc citizens.

The general indifference of the inefficient and uneducated leaders to the needs of the nation led to an incredible development of the nation's entrepreneurial skills, and he market thrived, with the US dollar becoming strong, and the main tender. In fact, there existed a chain of dollar shops, paradoxically set up by the government as their additional foreign currency income, where one could purchase foreign western goods for dollars! So much for socialist supremacy...

However, planning to travel west was quite complicated. One needed an official invitation from a foreign citizen of the country in question, guaranteeing accommodation and financial support during one's stay in his/her place.

Similar requirements were placed in front of future travellers by western countries, including the UK. Therefore, the whole process took a year. Six months waiting to obtain my passport, and another six to get my English visa... That said, the wait was worth every second and every penny!

London, here I come! After more than a decade of learning the language, from my childhood to my university years, I will be there! I never believed in learning spoken languages from books and local teachers. I've always felt that you have to feel and get to the place to be able to communicate effectively with native speakers. So I was on my way to fulfilling my biggest dream in the land of the 'Fab Four', as the Beatles were our idols and language guides, who we listened to during private parties with exceptional decorum. The forbidden fruit is always the sweetest...

The touchdown at Gatwick Airport had a very symbolic meaning; freedom at last! My life is my oyster from now on... After meticulous formalities, invitation presentations, and endless questions from the immigration control doubting Thomas', I stepped into my dreamland with a total of £4.65, not even enough to get a taxi from the airport to the town centre! The intention of this limit, introduced by the Polish government, was possibly intimidation and/or punishment tactics for abandoning the dear homeland to the benefit of the rotten western capitalists. Whatever the reason, any attempt to smuggle more would have been in vain - the goods would have been confiscated!

Fortunately, the stress was diminished by helpful friends - *nota bene*, half of my faculty made it to London at that time, and I was whisked away to the highly esteemed St. John's Wood district in the City of Westminster to my new abode. A strange little room in a strange little flat, with people speaking strange English! The landlady was Venezuelan, and her husband was English.

Initially, it seemed absurd. After all these years of studying English at home, and passing endless exams, I could not get it! This is the Cockney dialect for you! Even the evening ventures to the local pub turned out to be disastrous - full of 'apples and pears' (stairs) and referring to me as a snob for speaking proper English! Well, literary English, to be precise. Therefore, it was time to succumb to new pastures and change old habits!

Sweet revenge came soon enough, though. It was the famous 1973 World Cup qualifying match between the English and Polish football teams at Wembley. It cost the English a qualifying place, and later it was labelled "the death of football." It was my turn to laugh now and refute the Polish goalkeeper's and captain's descriptions as "clowns". The pub, this sacred abode of social life in this country, was in mourning, and the silly comments about my English ceased.

The average English classes that were offered widely to foreigners were simply boring. Then came the possibility of enrolment at the University of London, and the English teaching school that taught English at an advanced level. To ensure the extension of my six-month visa, which I was granted exceptionally as the aim of my visit was to master my English, I enlisted. And I kept reminding myself that the passport was only valid for two years.

As we were from the opposite political bloc, there were no means of financial support from the state, and we had to use our socialist ingenuity to survive. We were all in the same boat and supported each other as much as we could. Starting with sharing rented accommodation, job placements, and spare time...

I had to take various part-time jobs to allow myself to help make ends meet. In times of financial crisis, there was always a friend at a local Wimpy bar, ready to save me with unforgettable cheeseburgers and over-sweetened knickerbocker glories!

There were lots of us, all graduates from the same university group and full of expectations... Of what? We did not know. The contrast with life at home was quite striking. We abandoned the culture of daily long queues, rationed food, and continuous struggle for survival in a classless society that was based on the Orwellian version of the 'Big Brother watching'. And we landed as foreign individuals in this multinational beehive, full of diverse races, customs, religions, and outlooks on life. No more rows of shop shelves covered with packets of bay leaves and decorated with rows of bottles of vinegar.

We found an abundance of everything, in shops, the rush in the streets, freedom of speech and travel, and most importantly, self-determination!

Londinium, established in Roman times, was full of attractions, and we tried to taste them all. The star of them was the revolving restaurant at the then Post Office Tower. The panoramic views from this giant, where more than 14 million are surviving the beehive syndrome, were breathtaking, both day and night!

The hippie atmosphere was very strongly present everywhere. From Carnaby Street fashion with mini-skirts and platform shoes, to protest songs and CND (Campaign for Nuclear Disarmament) marches in the name of "Make love not war", as the Cold and Vietnam Wars were in full swing. How optimistic we were...

The long-studied history and traditions were everywhere to be seen. From the Big Ben bell, chiming every quarter of an hour at the top of the Elizabeth Tower over the Houses of Parliament, to Westminster Abbey, full of influential people's graves, tombs and plaques. From Elizabeth I, Dickens, Darwin, Livingstone, Newton and Hawking, just to name a few. The tube system was a total novelty and surprisingly easy to manage. Trafalgar Square and its surrounds, impressed with its Victorian grandiosity, and double-deckers allowed perfect sightseeing trips all over the metropolis at a minimal cost.

The city, with its army of civil servants in pinstriped suits, bowler hats, and banking fraternity, flocked every day to the square mile of the European financial heart. In addition, the Thames, running across this giant, offered an easy way to admire the 2000 years of growth and power of this amazing cosmopolitan hub. It felt like the place was for taking!

First Steps Outside London

Life continued with the usual ups and downs, and was never uneventful. Friends came and went. Some went back home, and some moved on in the western direction. I worked in various places, getting to know the highs and the lows, the local milkman and the self-made millionaire, wondering about emptiness in some people's lives, and the way money can make or break others.

The surroundings were also tempting. Many trips outside London gave me confidence and knowledge about the local geography, history, and fascinating architecture. My travelling bug took me to the south of the country. As my finances were very limited at that time, I decided to hitchhike for a week from Eastbourne to Southampton. It all started very positively, and helped me to make a new discovery. My favourite village of Alfriston, a neolithic settlement which became famous for smugglers sent to Australia as a punishment, and ghosts... Hidden with its Tudor houses, peace, and mother nature to shelter it. And not far from the most famous chalk hilltop formation, the Seven Sisters, overlooking the English Channel. Bliss... and a setting for many a film.

After a week of exploring, chatting to the locals, and breathing the sea air, I felt revitalized and ready to return to the Old Smoke - a nickname given to London due to its infamous smog which engulfed the capital in Victorian times, thanks to millions of fireplaces gushing smoke through the chimneys.

My adventure was coming to an end. I reached historic Southampton. From the Stone Age until now, it has been considered a very important port, bidding farewell to many, including the "unsinkable" Titanic. The island, not too far away, the Isle of Wight, was tempting and bidding... So, I decided to make it a final stopover.

The ferry docked on the shore in the middle of nowhere. An old, dilapidated Morris Minor stopped by my side. I had a look and was completely lost. I heard, "Do you speak English?" The voice enquired from within... "From time to time," was my reply, followed by an offer of a lift. I looked inside the car; one Aussie in a cork hat, one Geordie (the north of England tribe near Newcastle), one Kiwi, and one Irishman. What a mixture of worldly guys... I accepted the offer of the lift.

And so, my new cultural enrichment began. First, we went to the pub, of course. Then we did a round of mini golf outside on the lawn. I held "the stick", as I called it, the wrong way, which made them all roll with laughter on the green... another lesson learnt! In the evening, we set up camp, sat by the fire, and sang with the Irishman playing his guitar till the early hours of the morn...

We sang all the songs we could remember, including the ones of my idols, The Beatles, which we followed religiously as teenage rebels in Poland during private parties. This subversive music was not to the authorities' liking. Wrong role models... Such a deja vu in the land of the four. The mood changed rapidly in the morning, when we discovered that we had set up the camp next to the cemetery!

Back in London, things went back to normal. I met the Geordie, once in the nearby local in Knightsbridge, then again in the more classy Hilton tearoom in Park Lane, but it was not his day.

The impressive arrival outside the hotel in his cream convertible Jaguar XJ S was overshadowed by the direct refusal of the beast to start its engine when it was time to depart. I ended up pushing the car to a side road. What a first date! And how beneficial for my muscle power!

The time came to renew my visa requiring a visit to the Home Office in Croydon. The foreigners willing to study were favoured and I was given an extended permit to stay allowing me to continue to explore HM Land for another six months!

My Initial Observations

It was different, attractive, steeped in traditions and attention to detail with a touch of a relaxed approach to all around us, and certainly to the rest of the world. Even TV transmissions focused mainly on the English-speaking countries battling for power and recognition. The European flavour was absent in that decade, including Eastern Europe as well as the wild unknown USSR, seen as threatening and guilty of demonizing, terrorizing, and submitting millions of people to blind obedience in the name of the working people for the working people.

This bipolar paranoia was ludicrous. On one side, the Western Front, with more or less supportive Americans hoping to rule the world in everything, including space, and on the other, well-educated but certainly poorly aware - or frightened - nations of the rest of the world. While in Poland, many of us benefited from the keen services of Radio Free Europe and, for the young ones, Radio Luxemburg - if lucky, as the transmitters were interfered with buzzing noises during programmes; we called them bees.

But generally, the media was full of party propaganda, overfed and over- friendly simpletons, embracing and kissing in front of the Populus in the name of artificially imposed friendship and mutual adoration. And to think that the show and its ideals captured the imagination of the leading brains of this country, including the intellectuals from the Loxbridge triangle, ie London, Oxford, and Cambridge universities.

With time, the initial shock and realisation that I was actually "on the other side" eased off and I decided that the political realities of it all were beyond me. Life was good. I enjoyed what I was given one day at a time, and did not worry about tomorrow.

And as life is like a box of chocolates - you never know what you get - my special choccy was on its way...

Back to the Continent

While studying in Warsaw, I worked for a student travel agent who gave me a rare opportunity of direct contact with western youth. They were groups mostly from England and Spain - excellent practice for a linguist! One group, especially, was to make a mark on my life. It it was a group of medical students from Zaragoza, Spain. They were fun from the moment we met at Warsaw airport, cheerful, with bags of humour, Sangria, positive thinking, and... ladies' knickers! Yes, knickers, as they heard that they were the best commodity to trade on the black market in Poland - because of shortages - with an exorbitant profit! I could not confirm that the reality was as such - it was too embarrassing - but any foreigner could actually dispose of all his belongings and much-in-demand US dollars at unheard-of rates.

My next life chocolate appeared in the form of a letter sent to me by my medic friend from that group. His cousin worked in Barcelona and needed a Polish translator. What a great chance to experience new territories! But they were unaware of the political nuisances and Polish bureaucratic restrictions. Such positions were only awarded to high-level party members - I was not one of them. So after making some diplomatic phone calls, we decided I would work for them in secret - any formal visits from the Polish authorities would be dealt with without me.

The prospect of working in Barcelona seemed unreal... After over a year in England, my Spanish was getting rusty, and the technical nature of the project was totally unfamiliar. Still, I decided to give it a go. Soon, the ticket arrived courtesy of the firm EYSSA, and I was off to yet another stopover on my extended western holiday!

¡Hola Barcelona!

Interestingly, on my arrival, I experienced another linguistic hurdle. Barcelona is the capital of Cataluna, and the Catalans are extremely nationalistic! They all communicate in Catalan and sneer at the

Spanish speakers - only my status as a Polish foreigner excused me from this obligation, and I could speak Spanish!

The weather was unusually unwelcoming; dry and hot, sending one to sleep at 2pm after lunch and a glass of Vino Tinto. The concept of Spanish siesta became clear! However, traditional office hours prevented me from joining the others in this clever tradition, and I had to keep awake, resorting to a carajillo (a strong espresso with a drop of brandy/whisky) a day as I was really sleepy, and it was hot, hot, hot...

The weekends were well-spent, on the beach, and sightseeing with my housemates. One Catalan, one Swedish, one Colombian, and one Spanish, but no male companions were allowed on the premises. Imagine my shock when I discovered that one had a married lover of five years, one was pregnant, and the other was going out with two or three blokes concurrently! And I was wondering whether inviting my male friend from England for a coffee would have caused a revolution...

Yes, Ken the Geordie visited me and stayed in a hotel in La Rambla, the famous walking strip leading from the town centre to the statue of the proud Colon (Christopher Columbus), pointing to the west by the seafront. The place is famous for everything colourful, starting with masses of beautiful canaries, flowers, plants, immobile statues, jugglers, magicians, and artists.

I spent the whole week exploring the Medieval Quarter and its restaurants with the Els 4Gats - the hub of painters old and new - Gaudi, Casal, Picasso on the priority list, followed by Sagrada Familia (more than 135 years in the making designed by the genius

Gaudi), famous Barceloneta beach, and obviously the Camp Nou - the cradle of Barcelona FC.

After Ken left reality hit again and I returned to work. One weekend, my Spanish friend invited me to visit his hometown of Teruel in the Aragon province. It is very secluded and nicely hidden in the undulating, yellowish mountains famous for its tragic love story, reminiscent of the Romeo and Juliet plight in Verona, but with a more dramatic ending. The exodus was a joint suicide.

It was my only opportunity to taste the rural, traditional, and professional family life - away from the tourist-maddening crowds. Quiet, respectful, and set in its ways, as was the dinner I was invited to with the china crockery, silver cutlery, and two servants at each end of the table. An amazing experience for someone who saw such splendid occasions only in Hollywood classics!

And as powerful as the one of an emergency visit my doctor friend had to pay to a frail old lady in the nearby village at dusk. The contrast between afternoon wealth and evening basics was overwhelming. Those small, humble figures clad in black dresses and head covers, living in simple, sandy dwellings...

Back in Barcelona, my contract was coming to an end. It was yet another enriching experience with occasional linguistic battles and challenges to avoid the Polish delegations of party bigwigs. As I was practically non- existent, I had to make myself scarce on many occasions.

It was also the time of my big life dilemma. Shall I pack and go back home, knowing perfectly well that it would have been the end of my adventure, or return to England, as my visa and my passport were still valid for a while? Ken was very keen to see me again in London, and I was quite keen to see him and London again. So, after some visa problems, I bid adios to Spain down at a rainy Heathrow.

Back in London

Hampstead, Maida Vale, Highgate, and finally Bayswater near Hyde Park. Somehow things developed very nicely between us, and we decided to try it together... Life was young and carefree, full of plans, ideas, and the unknown. I decided to introduce my boyfriend to my parents. Of course, a visit to Poland was out of the question; I would not have been allowed to leave again. The only solution was to meet up somewhere else. And we did - in then-Yugoslavia. We met in sunny Dubrovnik and the National Park of Plitvice with its famous waterfalls. After a week, we parted - they went back to Poland by coach, and we hitch-hiked across Europe. Forty-two hours in the pouring rain, coming across all types of people. From the Turkish driver of a banger without windscreen wipers, who was wiping the screen with his arm, at full speed, to the hyper-sporty BMW owner who felt so sorry for the two lost sheep soaked in the pouring rain that he offered us his "humble" abode. A hyper-modern house with all its technical gadgetry. We spent a night in it and were fed German delicacies. Life is full of surprises!

Another Big Decision Time

And they continued. We were getting married! Thet radition was going to be altered due to the world political divide. None of my family members was able to come. I was the only representative of my entire brood at the Catholic church ceremony witnessed by the Anglican congregation in South Shields in the north of England!

How bizarre! In addition, the guy who gave me away was my fiance's uncle, who was Norwegian! And the whole occasion was planned according to the English tradition!

Well, the dress I bought in the Pronuptia store in Oxford Street was a medieval white gown with a hood and trumpet sleeves finished with a fury trim; like Snow White and Audrey Hepburn in one. Everything went smoothly, and everybody enjoyed the occasion and the local customs. After two days, we returned to London, facing life together. In other words, Ken went back to his accounting job at Conoco multinational petrol enterprise, and I went back to my job as a personal assistant in an insurance company in the City. Yet another interpersonal experience with a boss who knew nothing about his job. I had to grind my teeth and smile...

Back in Bayswater

Married life started on a very good footing. Both of us were working, enjoying the challenges of sharing everything and looking forward to the future. We lived in a rented studio flat in a very affluent area, full of interesting encounters and surprises. The community spirit was very strong then. Every Saturday, we used to walk to the Hungarian Bakery and indulge in their heavenly rye bread and cakes, like no other... Hyde Park was attractive any time of the year and week. Our swimming pool was around the corner, and the department store Whiteley's, with its Victorian decor, was a great spending magnet.

The place was teeming with very rich Arabs who used to walk in the main street, followed at a distance by three or four ladies clad in black capes and head covers. Some even covered their faces so one could only see their eyes... The reaction was that of bewilderment. Only with time, I understood the meaning of the attire and its cultural origins. The degree of female subservience stunned me, as I was brought up in a socialist society of nearly equal rights for both men and women. Poor - no, not poor, but just the opposite - extremely wealthy but oppressed - souls...

Our First Baby Is Joining Us!

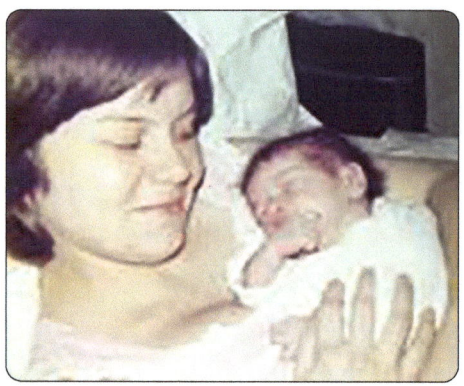

Caroline - my Sweetie - arrived a year-and-a-half later at St. Mary's Hospital, Paddington, famed for the discovery of penicillin. She was a bouncy, inquisitive bundle of joy who walked at nine months, and was a delight to everyone who met her. I enjoyed watching her grow and achieve her developmental milestones at an accelerated rate! After a while, we started to enjoy the attractions for children in Hyde Park. The international company was very stimulating and allowed me to learn different styles and approaches to children's upbringing. One of the kids in the sandbox impressed me immensely. He was only four years old, and fluent in French with his mother, Arabic with his father, and English with his peers in the playground – an early multilingual!

In the meantime, an opportunity arose to purchase a newly decorated maisonette in a beautiful street nearby full of Georgian houses, which were converted into flats.

The daily exercise of carrying my bundle of joy and her pram to the third floor did us a lot of good. Life was peaceful and quite organized until the Linguaphone Institute approached me as a linguist to co-write a new Polish language course for English speakers!

I could not believe my luck! Of course I couldn't! So the contract was signed, and the work began. Never in my entire life had I suffered such headaches and migraines. This, yet another, challenge was a real Mt. Everest! To include all of the Polish grammar in 30 lessons could not be possible! But I succeeded! My pride and patience were suffering gravely, but in the end, the course was published with great pomp in London - another mission accomplished.

Another Life-Changing Event

All that in addition to a fantastic possibility of spreading my linguistic wings and acquiring another profession. I applied to the School for the Study of Human Communication in Blackfriars, and was offered an interview by a delightful and open-minded lady, Margaret Fawcus, who listened to me, and much to my surprise, offered me a place on a two-year course. "If you do three years in two, the diploma is yours." She opened the world gates for me, for which I am eternally grateful, and I managed to contact her decades later to thank her again for her apolitical and humane approach to me, allowing my professional progress. The offer was possible to accept because the first year covered most of the subjects I did at Warsaw University. I was a Polish graduate, and it was not very politically correct to allow me to study at an English university! I was elated and learned another lesson in my life on English soil; where there is a will, there is a way, and all obstacles can be overcome - even the political ones! I was in, and for two solid years, I studied every day from 9am to 5pm, while my precious Sweetie (thank you, Neil Diamond, for Sweet Caroline) was being entertained, and entertained her peers and staff at the local private nursery. Getting up early, enjoying the ride on mum's bike, to be dropped off at the stimulating paradise for a full day! And mum, struggling through London on the London Underground, which was always packed and full of the whole world representatives! A mini-United - more or less - Nations.

It was worth it - the diploma opened a new professional world to me, and international gates were also opened - the demand for speech and language therapists has always been enormous...

Very Much-Needed Breaks

Holidays were necessary due to the intensity of life. We made our breaks in the beautiful Polish and unspoilt lake district that was recently declared a UNESCO World Heritage Site. We visited spectacular Polish mountain ranges and explored the Mediterranean basin. We also tried the Italian Alps in Sauze de Oulx near Sportinia, skiing at 2000m, and loved it there for the hospitality, forests, and fresh air... Quite a change from central London.

The biggest attraction was Greece and its archipelago of islands. We packed the backpacks and flew to Athens, and from there, we followed the island- hopping route. From Piraeus port to Paros, Antiparos, and Mykonos - all volcanic gems with individual treasures and customs. The final destination was Samos, the only green island close to Turkey with a hilly landscape, lush greenery, and empty, sandy beaches. What a place to relax! We set up our tent right on the beach, and every evening climbed the dunes and studied the spectacular star show. If it rained, the alternative was a nearby cave, the most uncomfortable sleeping experience I had ever endured. But the adventure was intoxicating... that's when we realized we had caught the travelling bug, and I developed a taste for Metaxa, the amber Greek spirit brewed by Spyros Metaxa in Samos since 1888. The combination of local Muscat wines and Mediterranean botanicals was unique and exquisite.

The biggest discovery in our search for relaxing places was Tunisia, which I first visited with Caroline before the other treasures were born. We flew to Tunis and were taken by coach to the village of Skanes near Sousse. The hotel on the beach was unexpectedly and totally family-oriented, with a clientele from all over Europe. The exotic food, warm air, and endless activities were exhilarating. From horse riding on the beach to sailing the sea, be it in a pirate ship, or a speedy motorboat, which often took us far out and introduced us to a novel way of catching octopuses in clay pots sunk at the bottom of the sea and marked at the top with plastic mini-buoys. From paragliding (our everyday must, as the views are unforgettable and the silence up there is deafening!), to joining the camel caravans and visiting Bedouin tents and tasting their clay oven-baked bread. From visiting the jewel of Tunisian heritage Bardo Museum in Tunis, with the most impressive collection of artefacts as the intact Roman mosaics, to the El Jem amphitheatre in the south of the country, built as a replica of the Colosseum in Rome, and fully preserved under the auspices of UNESCO - quite a treat! Further south, we enjoyed the troglodyte structures in Matmata, where the Berber tribe lives, and it was chosen for filming some of the Star Wars episodes. The country became our regular two-yearly destination for more than 20 years - the best holiday spot for us for many, many reasons... And, unfortunately, out of bounds for us since 2010 as it was in SidiBou Said – a white and blue house settlement - where the Arab spring started with a young activist setting himself alight in a protest against corruption and economic stagnation of the regime. It spread over five Arabic countries, and Tunisia is still a hub for the extremist movement.

As the situation in the country was getting tense with the decisions implemented by Margaret Thatcher, information about strikes and overall discontent took over the newspaper front pages.

We decided to sell our home and travel to New Zealand. The perspective of moving to pastures new and facing different lifestyles and cultures was so exciting! Going half around the world and stopping over in as many countries as was practical was beyond a dream come true! My travelling bug was awakened yet again then, and it has stayed with me forever.

We could not travel to Poland to say goodbye to my family, so my parents were invited to join us for Christmas. The formal invitations were duly submitted to the Passport Office in Warsaw, and they awaited the release of the passports. It was taking a suspiciously long time. In the end, my father phoned and informed me that the passports were declined without explanation. No one knew what was brewing. Two days later, they declared a state of emergency in Poland, and the army tanks filled Warsaw. We were devastated, worried, and uncertain of future developments.

Christmas was gloomy, stressed, and busy with packing the crates to be shipped to Auckland. We had all the vaccines necessary in Asia and Australasia, and at the end of January, we left for our trip of a lifetime! With a carefully prepared set of study books for Caroline to follow the English curriculum, as she was going to miss quite a few months of her formal education - the informal one was ahead of us!

CHAPTER 2

WE ARE OFF TO SEE THE WORLD!

T he adventure started in the early morning of a very frosty day. The pavements were covered with a two-inch layer of solid ice - a semi-ice-skating rink...

Gatwick was buzzing as usual, and our 14-hour flight to stage one of the trip to Colombo via Zurich - Dubai - Karachi was delayed by one hour. I was worry-ridden about the situation in Poland and the family's status quo. *The Times* published a map of Poland with its eastern border lined with Russian tanks. It looked bad. The whole country was cut off from the outside world.

The communication system was closed, so I decided to try the obvious. They must allow a telegram, as it implies some kind of emergency. It worked, they got it, and I am still looking at it as an especially sentimental memento - a beginning of a new life for us and for them in every new sense of the word. And there is a blue stamp on it - as on all envelopes sent to them from our journey - the ominous CENSORED.

The stopover in Dubai taught me that I am not a fan of heat, and neither is my body. We were allowed off the plane for one hour. The moment I stepped out, I swelled doubly and could not walk but had to shuffle along the shops laden with every possible type and colour of gold - the wealth abundant...

Ambudayan Sri Lanka!

We landed in Colombo; our world was transformed by the hot breeze, coconut palm trees and masses of calm, smiling, and relaxed people who greeted us with both hands joined together at chest level saying "hello" in Singhala. We took a taxi to our pre-booked hotel and had a long, well- deserved nap. First lunch was a true culinary experience. I fell in love with a coconut curry. Even now, the taste lingers on – hot, but so smooth and exotic! And washed down with the obligatory king coconut water, directly from the fruit itself through a straw - mother nature at its best! Then we went out to book a one-week trip around the island.

Caroline decided she wanted to play in the sand on the beach, of course. She was also overwhelmed by the change in everything. So I hid in the shade, and she hoped to enjoy half-an-hour in the sun. The results were shocking.

Within minutes, she was covered with blisters, and the locals suggested placing her in the restaurant ice box where they kept fresh fish. She still remembers the smell... And I remember the sight of my daughter looking like an enlarged sheet of bubble wrap!

Lesson one: observe the locals and the local habits. Never transfer your learnt and well-established knowledge and behaviour directly into a new culture. It might cost you dearly, literally and metaphorically.

The next day we started our tour to the centre of the island to Kandy, the world heritage site established by UNESCO in 1988, and romantically placed in a valley by the lake, with its most famous sacred Buddhist Temple of the Tooth Relic. We drove through tea plantations, thick forests, endless displays of fantastically colourful flowers, and peaceful people often selling fresh coconuts, and even climbing the palm trees if you spotted one you really liked!

On the way, we saw a snake charmer with three cobras and three pythons, rode elephants, and were invited to a dance show and a Chinese feast in the local restaurant. And I could not stop admiring my replacement engagement ring (the original one was too big), which was an apparently rare blue topaz - my birthstone.

Also, the famous Botanical Gardens left a lasting impression. All kinds of palms, red banana, mahogany, almond trees - all 130 acres of tropical beauties, including a devil bush - the black, most intricate orchid ever seen. Caroline fitted in this exotic environment, becoming something of a point of interest to the natives - a young, white girl with insatiable energy.

And so my culture-enriching curve was rising steadily, learning every day about different outlooks on life, different religions, beliefs, customs, habits, cuisines, tribes, and their conflicts. Yes, Tamil

Tigers were in action in the north, fighting for their independence: the Hindu tribe with its own language and identity.

We could only tour half of the island and be fortunate to see its amazing riches and history. The land of 1001 smiles...

Sawasdee Thailand!

Air Lanka flew us to Bangkok. The service was royal, the stewardesses looked and behaved royally, and this new experience was so strong we even remember what was served on the flight.

Thailand continued with Asian hospitality and politeness, with a calm approach to life, even in stressful and detrimental situations. We stayed in the hotel overlooking the Royal Palace and the University. Our venture in the morning to the local market deafened our ears: noise, tuk-tuks (very well-ventilated three-wheelers with no windows, and capable of reaching the remote and secluded parts of the town), shouting sellers, and endless stands with every type of fare imaginable. What a contrast with peaceful Sri Lanka! And poverty was present everywhere... While 46 metres long and covered with 1.5 tonnes of pure gold Buddha has been reclining near the Palace since 1848...

We were treated to traditional touristy sights like the floating market full of long-tail-boats manoeuvring full of fresh fruit, trinkets, and goods of all sorts on the Chao Phraya River, like cars in the traffic jams in London. Folk shows with local delicacies and trips to various Buddhist temples. The land of 1001 trades, as everything seems to be produced in front of your eyes. All basic needs satisfied here and now!

It was time to chill and to change the scene, and we left for Pattaya - the centre of sunseekers and fun seekers. We tried paragliding, snorkelling, pedaloes, windsurfing, and whatever came our way...

I was still very worried about the developments in Poland and tried to phone them, and had no luck. But the receptionist in the hotel solved the problem using a linguistic excuse as a non-Polish speaker and putting me through to the Warsaw exchange. All I managed to ask was, "Is everything calm?" The answer was very reassuring yes. I could relax again...

After one week in this tropical paradise full of all good and bad, it was time to move on south.

Ni Hao Singapore!

Famous for its colonial Raffles Hotel and its two fan palms on each side of the entrance and the Singapore Sling - a cocktail of gin, Angostura bitter, and lime juice - initially served only at this hotel in the Long Bar, having been developed by its bartender in 1915. The tradition continues now, together with the accelerated price rise! But to be in Singapore and not try the Singapore Sling...?

We stayed in the Metropole next to the Raffles - affordable and less posh, with clientele from every corner of the world.

The republic is very Western European, clean and organized, with no slums and people looking content - strikingly content. No chewing gum was and is allowed on the island, so cleaning the white pavements becomes a doddle...

The Lion City is mostly Buddhist but is declared the world's most religiously diverse place. Its extremely important strategic location makes it a centre of trade for all and sundry in the East.

Time was short and we had to continue moving South, bidding goodbye to this well-governed island; the post-colonial jewel welcoming and respecting the world's diversity.

Halo Indonesia!

Singapore Airlines flew us to Jakarta. The service was second to none. We were treated with a smile, calm and Asian warmth... not to mention the food treats...

Jakarta was a total shock. From Singaporean civilisation, we landed in a dingy hotel in the middle of town and watched some kids blowing up live frogs across the road. The hotel sheets were stained, and the staff were arrogant. Good job we had only a couple of nights to endure.

With "never again", we flew to Bali to spend a real week off to enjoy the sand and the sea. From the Denpasar airport, we were taken to Sanur beach - the second most famous among the backpackers passing by via the island, on the way to any destination in the world. The first place was taken by Kuta beach, full of Aussies on their way to the Old Motherland, or on the way back home. Excited, noisy and buzzed up.

Sanur was calm, relaxed, and more traditional. The Gazebo hotel offered us a bamboo hut with a terrace and balcony opposite the swimming pool. Caroline was in her element. Any mention of schoolwork was refuted with an offer to cool down in the pool. It was really hot and humid, and the monsoon was adding insult to injury - nothing was dry! We could not wear our clothes as everything was damp or soaked. Even the geckoes stopped visiting, hiding in the jungle in despair.

The place was very peaceful, and the people were happy living life as they preached. It felt very spiritual and in unison with nature. All the live folk shows tackled the concept of the struggle between good and bad. And some showed a trance dance telling a local love story, reflecting positivity and unity with one another and mother nature. All that was among forested volcanic mountains, paddy fields, stunning beaches, and coral reefs. A paradise for the body and the soul...

G'day Australia!

One big jump over the equator and we landed in Sydney after a four-hour flight. The heat was unbearable, and so was the humidity. This melting pot of all nationalities under the sky is fascinating and resembles London. A short tour of the city and its architectural structures, including The Opera House and the Harbour Bridge, and a glance at Bondi Beach was exhausting enough. We hired a car and aimed for Newcastle - we were invited to visit a friendly couple we met in London. The views along the coastline were breath-taking: lots of space, beaches, nature reserves, mountains, and lakes... The heat was wearing us out, but we could not risk a splash in the sea - too dangerous because of subcurrents, jellyfish, stonefish and sharks...

Newcastle is situated on the Hunter River and has a lot to offer. We stayed there for a fortnight and looked for work and house opportunities. There were two buts to consider. The place is ridden with many creepy crawlies, which are safer to avoid, and everybody used their cars to move about... I could not drive! So, the final stop needs to be as planned - Auckland, here we come!

Kia Ora New Zealand!

After a month-and a-half, we arrived in the most spread-about city in the world - the most populous and multicultural in New Zealand, located on 48 volcanic cones. The youngest - only 600 years old in Rangitoto Island overlooking a spectacular panorama of the city, its Mission Bay and the yachts' galore, Sky Tower and all the volcanic hills constituting this enchanting and mysterious place.

We stayed in Epsom first with Ken's friends and enjoyed getting to know the place, customs, and environs - essential to its vibrant, young, and sporty population. After a while, we moved to a bungalow in One Tree Hill - the Maori hub with all the outdoor pastimes imaginable. I took some interest in archery at the weekends. The rest of the time, I looked for work, ferried Caroline to school, and decided I had to have a go at driving... on the "wrong" side of the road...

The beginnings were fantastically promising: I found two part-time jobs in local hospitals - one leading a dementia unit, and the other in the stroke clinic - a fascinating challenge! I love anything to do with neurology, so I was in my element...

Caroline was thriving at school, developing her exceptional dancing skills - and proving them in many shows, including "Fame", and loving the new stable life. Her life-learning curve was rising slowly, and the new experiences were very educational. She found NZ$10 in the famous Botanical Gardens to keep and spend as she wished - first budgeting lesson - and she was made to return a hair bobble, which she appropriated in a gift shop, to the shop assistant with apologies - her cardinal sin repented... Life was good. We managed to re-establish contact with my family by phone and by letters - all censored as usual.

In the meantime, New Zealand accepted 120 Polish families from the Vienna camps set up for the refugees following the fall of the Solidarity movement and the military takeover in Poland. They were very carefully chosen for their suitability to work in NZ. Singles, couples, and families, needing help and moral support. So, I made myself useful and met with some of them socially, interpreted for them, and generally established contact with the souls so far from their roots... I knew the feeling... it was very far away, and so different from Europe. The distance was palpable...

Our small home was a traditional colonial house with a tangerine bush by the terrace entrance. Much to my daughter's delight and astonishment that her lunch fruit could be picked from the garden, not from a shop!

The attractions around Auckland were unusual and intriguing... Starting with prehistoric-looking tree ferns, thick bushes, bottle brush trees, and endless beautiful flowers. From Cape Reinga -the most north-western tip of the island and the underworld for all souls according to Maori beliefs - to Wellington, the buzzing capital.

Everywhere we travelled, we were in awe - what a place! You could ski on Mt Ruapehu (an active stratovolcano that last erupted in 2007) in the morning and then sail away into the horizon in the afternoon across the Mission Bay past Rangitoto Island - the graceful cone emerging from the ocean with the world-famous largest forest of exotic New Zealand Christmas trees - Pohutukawa and numerous bird species, and ferns. A paradise reserve free of pests...!

Then came a visit to Rotorua - something of a scary geothermal place full of hissing vents with sulphuric steam, bubbling muds, and volcanic dens, not to mention a 30m tall Pohutu geyser entertaining tourists with its frequent eruptions.

Next, novelty awaited us in the spell-binding Waitomo Caves, with its underground river decorated with stalactites and galaxies of glow worms. The view is unforgettable, especially when seen in total silence - like watching the sky on a clear night through a telescope...

The kiwi adventure, with all its idiosyncrasies, left a very solid imprint on our memories - so different, so picturesque, and so diverse in every sense of the word. Maori heritage, Christmas turkey dinner on the beach in full sunshine, kiwi birds, varied flora, water sports, fern forests, volcanic formations, yet sooo far... away from our culture, customs, and habits...

After a year, it was time to bid the Island goodbye and move on to pastures new. I discovered something new about myself - yet again - that I am definitely a European citizen.

After a year, the crates had to be packed again and ready to be shipped back to England, and I had recurring regretful thoughts about leaving this unique place and looking forward to the second leg of our trip - returning to England via Tahiti and across the USA.

CHAPTER 3

FOUR MONTHS LONG TRAVEL HOME...

Our camper - our pride and joy while travelling in Mexico and across the USA

Tahitian beauties

Five hours later, having crossed the time zone, we landed in the French Polynesian Archipelago of the Society Islands in the capital Papeete. Discovered by Captain Cook, mountainous, bathed in lush greenery, and incredibly colourful. Our first decision was to explore the Island, and we caught the bus going somewhere... The novelty of the place, with its indefinite variety of unknown plants, flowers, and trees, captivated us. When the time came to rest our overheated bodies, nothing was available. It was only thanks to the local hospitality that we were offered a room to stay overnight by a local major who took pity on the three lost sheep and invited us to his house.

Tahiti's sister island is Moorea - a gracious extinct volcano crowned with two peaks towering over the pineapple plantations and pristine blue waters of the atoll. They say that it inspired Darwin, who visited and studied the islands, to propose his theory about their formation. To get there, one needs a ferry, and the crossing is the most violent I have ever experienced, and is considered the most perilous in the Pacific Ocean - all crew and passengers suffered from sea sickness - the ocean has its own agenda...

And finally, yet another tropical jewel - Bora Bora. Surrounded by sand- fringed islets and a turquoise lagoon protected by a coral reef – a scuba diver's paradise. Everywhere we looked, it was a postcard picture. Gauguin swapped western civilization for the beauty of the place, escaping Europe which made him sick! And he managed to reflect the Tahitian ambience in the synthetic style of his artworks.

One cannot dispute his choice, although there was one problem - especially for the travellers on a budget - as the islands are extremely costly... We lived mostly on French sticks and pineapples - a healthy, local diet. Mother nature's recipe.

It was time to go further West - to the land of milk and honey...

Hey USA!

Complete change of everything: climate, culture, customs, people, and colours. An eight-hour flight took us to LAX in Los Angeles. No more heat exhaustion, familiar set-up and transport, with new challenges to find an apartment and a means of transport to take us right across this vast country to New York.

The first day was interesting. The rented flat was fairly central, but we needed to explore possibilities in the area and needed a rent-a-car. So we hired a small (!) compact local family saloon and parked it outside. Much to our surprise - or rather shock - the next morning, the car was gone! Bewildered, we walked to the hire place just to hear, "Oh, it's nothing - it happens all the time" Welcome to America!!!

Another surprise awaited in the local fast food bar Wendy's. The portions were massive, and came with a generous serving of chips or, rather, French fries, using the local version... We could not eat the meals in full! So, the economical approach was applied - one for two, and we stuck to it throughout the American adventure.

It started with the purchase of a camper, a truck with an attachable living section that contained three beds, a table, and a basic kitchen section - small but comfortable, and detached at will if needed, to be able to use the truck. A clever little home on wheels. It was to take us on a four-month journey, and it never failed. Fortunately...

We started in LA, amazed by the vanity of Hollywood and its stars, and visited Universal Studios, Hollywood, and the compulsory Disneyland in Anaheim. Then South to Santa Ana, remembering not to miss the Christ Cathedral - the largest glass construction of that time accommodating more than 2,000 worshippers, and inspiring them with music coming from the largest pipe organ in the world during the tele-evangelisation masses, which reached more than 65 million viewers.

Then, on to San Diego, with its famous recreational Balboa Park, Sea World, and many, many local attractions. Then to Joshua Tree National Park, and all the way up north on County 101. On the way, we stopped in Santa Cruz at the Mystery Spot, a gravitational anomaly defying all laws of physics. We experienced puzzling variations of gravity, perspective, and height - all apparently due to a meteorite that landed there in ancient days. The gravity hill was discovered in 1939 in the California Redwood Forest and remains a prime curious attraction. It is a tilt-induced visual illusion as the oddly tilted environment causes misperceptions of the height and orientation of the objects in the tilted house. The balls roll uphill, and people lean further than normally possible without falling down! This piece de resistance of the local phenomena is located near San Francisco - the jewel of the western Pacific coast.

Originally called San Pancho, but renamed Yerba Buena – the name of a mint plant the Spanish explorers found growing on the shores, which translates to "good herb" – was a very interesting discovery and recognition of its properties – repeated recently by the Californian Government by legalising marijuana... They know the good stuff!

The current name was assigned to the town in 1848 in reference to St. Francis of Assisi, the patron saint of animals and nature.

The SF motto - Gold in Peace, Iron in War – a special appreciation of the allure of the Golden Gate and the Bay. The city was full of surprises hidden all over the hills. The Frisco Bay (Otis Redding sang about it, too), the famous last manually-operated cable cars conquering even the steepest routes, the enormity of Golden Gate Bridge opened in 1937, which is the longest and the widest suspension bridge in the world. Painted in its characteristic orange international colour, it is the most photographed construction in the world. The challenge of driving down the winding Lombard Street ,the strange attraction of Alcatraz Island and its prison, and the cosmopolitan atmosphere spreading all over the place... Loved it! Even the seafood was amazing. Although my conversion was not total...

Next, we drove to Sacramento - the official capital of California. It welcomed us with a Gold Rush atmosphere, with wagon rides, one-storey wooden buildings, and photo parlours where you could dress in late 19th- century attire and pose as a gold prospector and family in the Sierra Nevada mountains, stepping back in time to the days of the Pony Express mail-delivering service, and the first Transcontinental Railroad. From indigenous Nisenan and Madoc tribes all those centuries ago to the most "hipster city" in California. Also ranked as the most diverse in America.

Later we were in awe of Lake Tahoe- a complete change of climate and scenery, admiring the two million-year-old formation of the largest alpine lake in North America, situated on the border with Nevada, surrounded by forests, mountain ranges, and famous for its pristine waters. Nature at its best!

Back on the long, winding, and empty road, which is leading us to the Death Valley National Park, with the temperature reaching +55C, and its endangered pupfish, which only exists in this harsh environment considered the hottest in the world as well as Sahara and the Middle East deserts. The local Timbisha tribe of Native Americans has been inhabiting the hostile terrain for more than a millennium, and is still present in Furnace Creek – an oasis created by the hot water springs.

We cross the Nevada border , not knowing that a shock is awaiting us! We arrive in Las Vegas - the Sin City, and sinful it is... as one of the few places in the USA where gambling is permitted. It offers luxurious casinos full of punters playing everything from traditional roulette to some weird card games. The tables surrounded with people getting merry on free drinks, one-arm bandits – also known as the slot machines invented in 1898 in San Francisco - causing a racket, spitting out occasional monetary rewards.

Crowds of people everywhere hoping to make it in Las Vegas, including old biddies disposing of their husbands' fortunes, often spending the whole night hoping for the never coming fortune... The heat in the Nevada desert is unbearable, so the city found a solution to keep on attracting millions of visitors every year - they installed a sprinkler system in the main road named the Strip, so it is possible to cool down and continue exploring the architectural jewels. Like the Golden Nugget - the first-ever casino hotel and the upscale hyper-modern Wynn. The Venetian with its gondolas, Ceasar built in the fully Roman Empire style, Bellagio with its beautiful display of fountains dancing to the music, and Paris with a replica of the Eiffel Tower and the Montgolfier brothers' balloon.

Next, Flamingo Bay Resort, hosting famed singers all year round, and down the Strip, we visited New York - New York - the Big Apple-themed hotel with its rollercoaster. Luxor hotel was close by, with the replica of Sphynx guarding its entrance... And many more with multiple gambling and feeding attractions in each - all after your money...

The visit was a short study of human psychology and world riches. But mother nature offered a more exciting attraction. Created by millions of years of the Colorado River, which carved the red rock, revealing millions of years of geological history. And here was our first American surprise, the 500km long and 1.5km deep wonder of the world was filled with thick fog! We could only spot the highest peaks sticking out like cobblestones over the clouds.

The Arizona Desert visit had to be postponed... and we had to move south to pastures warmer. The idea of going to Mexico popped up, and it seemed like an exotic diversion from our route.

!Hola, Mexico!

We abandoned the hustle and bustle of California and Nevada, aiming to cross the border at Tijuana, famous for people smuggling and jazz bands. It was as busy as the Las Vegas strip, but soon we entered space and landscape seen in western films.

Undulating bare and sandy hills protected by massive elephant cacti able to live to 200 years and ingeniously adapted to the desert conditions, yucca trees, and blue Hesper palms decorating the arid land of the Baja California peninsula.

We decided to head south, passing through Ensenada, El Rosario, and Santa Rosalia all on the 500 km to Mulege following the Transpeninsular two-lane traffic road leading to the most southern tip in Cabo San Lucas. Hardly any people, a couple of gas stations, and dry wind... And an unexpected butterflies' attack, literally. A migrating swarm of monarchs hit our camper and nearly covered it on our way down south. There were many casualties, but we could not help it.

We had five-night stopovers before we found a place to stay in the middle of nowhere on the local beach, Santispac near Mulege - the place teeming with retired Americans in their campers enjoying the wilderness and peace. It was to be our stopover for two weeks - we found our long-awaited hot weather spot for the first time since leaving Tahiti.

Caroline was in her element. The beautiful bay offered safe swimming, colourful stones, shells of all kinds, and little time for homework. She had to be bribed to do her schoolwork (which I brought with us following the English curriculum publications so that she did not miss out on her education) with treat deprivation - the biggest being "No roast marshmallows for dessert."

We acquired the custom from the camping neighbours - the American standard sweet - perfect in these very restricted conditions.

Life was amazingly relaxed. In the morning, we had a swim with the pelicans. The shrimp boat visited us regularly, offering the freshest fruits of the sea. And in the evening, we had visitors every day - the vultures guarding any leftovers from our dinner. Tete-a-tete with mother nature in the full meaning of the word.

In addition, we met a guy who used to be an IBM CEO and resigned, then sold everything, and bought a yacht which he sailed up and down the Gulf of California. Named by Jacques Cousteau the aquarium of the world, it is visited by 85per cent of Pacific mammals. All types of whales, manta rays, turtles, dolphins, sharks, and sea lions, The captain took us on a couple of trips and thus confirmed. Oh, I do love to be sailing on the sea!

One Sunday, we went to the church in Santa Rosalia - just to be thrown out by an earthquake. It lasted only 30 seconds, but remains vivid in our memories. The feeling of complete disorientation and lack of experience in such situations bring about crowd panic. No direction to react sensibly, and loss of control.

In addition, we had to face some new challenges - finding edible pieces of meat, drinkable water, and vegetables... But they were nothing compared to this fantastic adventure shared with others in these unusual surroundings. What education for all of us! And the mementoes - the stones and shells from that beach, are still with me - the memories live on in England...

When the time came, we booked a ferry from Mulege to Guaymas and followed the only highway available via Nogales straight up north through Arizona back to the Grand Canyon.

Back in the USA

We drove on A17 through Tucson, Phoenix, and Flagstaff to the South Rim of the First Wonder of the world.

This time the welcome was truly hot. In fact, it was the hottest day of the year. The views were unforgettable. This red geological wonder changes colour all the time, revealing layer upon layer of fascinating patterns and shapes...

We walked the trail and decided to walk down into the Inner Canyon, beckoning with its arid atmosphere, and tempting the visitor with the promise of fresh water, the Colorado River right at the very bottom of this marvel. The river has been sculpting this unique formation for more than two billion years, and is still inhabited by the Arizonian indigenous tribes such as Navajo and Hopi. And many Californian condors show their prowess over the rocky wonder.

The views were changing all the time. Some people ventured on the donkey trail, but Caroline and I managed only the first station on the way to the river. It was scorching hot and very humid, affecting our breathing. My husband had a challenge streak in his veins, bid us goodbye, and went for a swim... He returned delirious, dehydrated, and exhausted at midnight. He was lucky: two other adventurers did not make it back. It was the hottest day in local history.

The next day we drove north to Utah, passing endless national parks and stopping in one of them, the Bryce Canyon - the most impressive after the Grand Canyon, with its white, orange, and red coloured spire-shaped rock formations, created by frost weathering and stream erosion of the river and lakebed sedimentary rocks - something unreal! Especially at sunrise and sunset... like in a fairy tale.

We hit State 70 in Salina and went east - in the direction of home...

From Utah - the Beehive State, through to Colorado - the Centennial State (named so to commemorate its inclusion into the states 100 years after the Declaration of Independence was signed in 1776) to Kansas - the Sunflower State, Arkansas - the Natural State bordering the Mississippi River, Montana - the Treasure State, Illinois - the Prairie State and the land of Lincoln, Indiana - the Hoosier State (the countrified one) and finally to Ohio - the Buckeye State named so thanks to the plentiful trees resembling the eye of a deer and the cradle of aviation thanks to the Wright Brothers. Later we followed State 71, taking us northeast - towards the Great Lakes...

We stopped briefly in Mansfield - famous for its first robot in the world and the film Shawshank Redemption. The reason for our visit was quite interesting. My father's best friend from WW2 times emigrated from Poland to the USA after the war and married there. Unfortunately, we were late in making it to meet him, but his wife was still alive and very moved when we arrived. She spent the whole time showing us endless mementoes and reminiscing...

Time was not on our side: we had to move on and followed the road from Pennsylvania to New York State. Soon, we arrived at yet another wonder of the world, on the American-Canadian border, joined by the Rainbow Bridge, Niagara Falls. This geological formation was created 10,000 years ago by glaciation, and its name originates in the local Niagagarega tribe - the power of nature at its best! Not to mention the enormous influence of its uniqueness on tourism, art, literature, cinematography, and human endeavour. Twelve people jumped and survived the fall, many using various gadgets to protect themselves from the 51m downward journey. Current law prohibits any attempt to cross the Falls.

The experience left us breathless and promising to return to this visually stunning, climatically unpredictable, and purely overpowering site. The frequent mist added mystery to this place, receding slowly towards Lake Erie, and doomed to disappear in 50000 years...

Bidding goodbye to this very real natural gem, we drove southeast towards our final destination, New York. On the way, we passed various American curiosities; fast food bars, motels, ice-cream parlours, and a small town called Warsaw in Wyoming, a place very close to my heart for obvious reasons. I was intrigued and toured this small piece of Polish tradition so far away from its roots! They say there are as many Poles outside Poland as in it. And one can take a Pole out of Poland, but cannot take Poland out of a Pole...

Well, here we were in the agricultural (dairy farming and maple syrup production) and manufacturing centre known for its salt and knitting mills. A quaint, traditional, time-forgotten settlers' town. Very American...

We were approaching the end of our adventure, but before we reached Empire City, we diverted to Doylestown, Pennsylvania, for a very specific reason. The town was established in 1745 and is steeped in history, not only in the American but also in the Polish one. The local Catholic church is a shrine to the Black Madonna of Czestochowa, and its stained-glass windows depict Polish history from the pagan beginnings to modern times - all of its 1000 years of rich and often tragically eventful past, including those who made Poland count in the world: astronomer Copernicus, composer Chopin, pianist Paderewski, and endless historians, kings, academics, religious order founders. A really impressive and modern way of educating the visitors and the regulars. In all my travels, I have never seen such an object de art recalling historical events in hyper-modern technique on glass! Beauty and style at its best!

On to New York now. We sold the camper and decided to rent a car. The classic American Cadillac arrived in its full glory: smooth cruise control, allowing the car close to drive itself on the straight. The comfort was exceptional. It was nearly as good as sitting in an armchair, and the space inside was double our camper home.

So, we - or it? - drove all the way to John F Kennedy's airport near the Big Apple. Four months, 5000km, and 18 states later, our halfway round the world return home was nearing the end - or so we thought...

Having totally lost awareness of the real-world, we parked happily at the airport car park and went to search for the earliest flight back to London. We tried to get the tickets on a stand-by basis (the cheapest way to travel) only to discover that all 10 flights to England were fully booked as it was Independence Day in the USA and the whole nation was in a holiday mood and on the move!

God bless America! And its love for comfort. The Cadillac served as our lodgings for the next two nights - and finally, on the third day, we managed to get the tickets, and soon, we were on the plane going back to home sweet home in London...

Not ours, though, as we had nowhere to live, having sold our maisonette one-and-a-half years ago. My friend accommodated the three homeless lost sheep in her house in Chelsea, and so the adventure came to an end...

CHAPTER 4
BACK IN ENGLAND

Bassingbourn Sign

10th-century Church

The priority to find a house was urgent as I discovered, much to my delight, that I was pregnant. We were all excited but the reality was knocking at our door - we needed to buy a place and find jobs! So after moving to our friends' flat in North London, we contacted local estate agents who started sending us leaflets of houses past the green belt surrounding London. We were looking at properties in the northern direction and eventually moved into our new house in the South Cambridgeshire village of Bassingbourn, located in the middle of fields.

My Second Daughter's Arrival

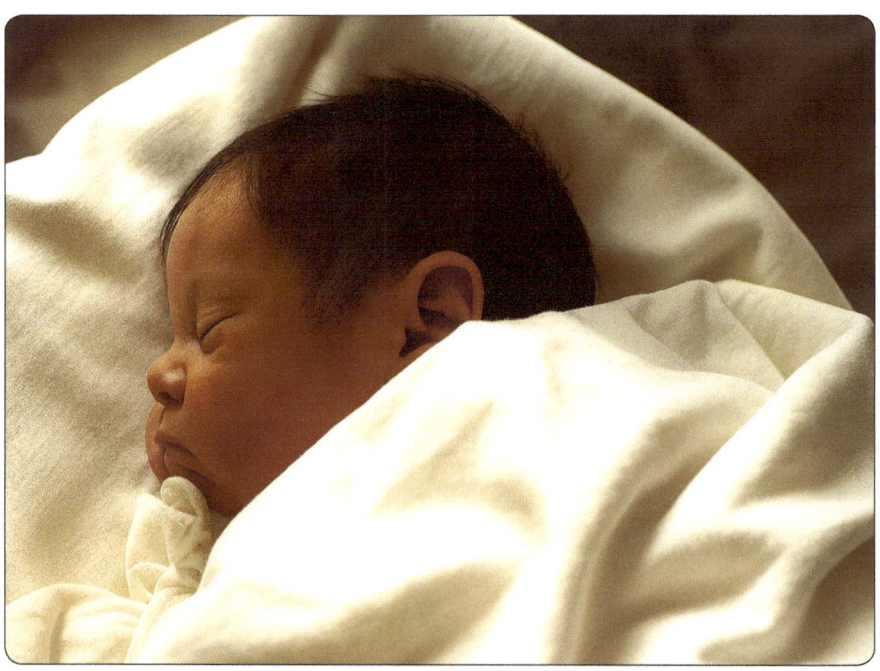

The crates sent from New Zealand by sea were delivered to our end-of-terrace three-bedroom house with a large garden and plenty of space. The village was very old and full of quirky history: the place was famous for locals heating their homes in the past with the local deposits of dinosaur dung. The first London taxis were made there in its iron works. Glenn Miller flew from the local airfield to disappear over the English Channel at the end of the WW2. And there were many, many other interesting stories...

My baby decided to arrive in the evening. All appeared to go well but, as usual, both of us worked hard and needed a well-deserved rest. The next day we were called to the consultant paediatrician's room and informed that following a blood analysis test, it was certain that my daughter had Down syndrome and we "don't have to take her home as she will not do anything anyway."

The attitude shocked me. As a speech therapy student I had my practice sessions with these delightful, calm and observant people and I could not believe that a high-ranking professional in the leading teaching hospital - namely Addenbrooke's linked to Cambridge University - could be so bland and obviously cruel.

The baby was beautiful and peaceful. A little twinkling star... The latest addition to our family was certainly a challenge. Emma Kathrine was constantly sick and was not developing as expected. I spent months trying to feed her whatever would build her up but with no success. After a while, my local GP said, "put your ear to her chest - it's like Niagara Falls." Indeed, it was: they discharged my child with a gigantic heart problem - she had atrial and septal defects in her heart. They let us go home with Emma's life expectancy of a maximum three years! That is medical negligence at its worst.

So, the problem was to bring her weight up to the operable requirement and hope for the best at the best children's hospital in London in Great Ormond St. They were very open about the risks and did not raise our hopes. At the age of 14 months Emma underwent her operation and the surgeons were very pleased with the result, which was 80 per cent successful but for how long only time would show. What they achieved was close to a miracle; after two weeks in an induced coma, and some additional complications which required surgical intervention, Emma came home after one month.

Life in Bassingbourn

My husband Ken found a job in London with one of the petrol companies, which made him a classic commuter: early rise, hop in the car, and drive to Royston - a town three miles away with a railway station - catch the train to London and after all day in the capital return stressed back home - only to have dinner and repeat the schedule day after day ...

Caroline was very happy to have a sister. She joined the local school and was thriving in everything she touched. Her dancing was really exceptional, her piano recorder exam results spoke for themselves, her sports day participation was always rewarded for athletic achievements, and she was very sociable.

Emma was developing at the normal rate now and there was a definite need for social contact with her peers. I approached the local council, suggesting that she joined our local nursery twice a week with a supporter. I offered to pay for both, but was refused point-blank as "this is not the policy of this council." I did not give up, and - being used to jumping the red tape in Poland - I continued fighting for her rights. Eventually, they surrendered and Emma joined the local group with a helper.

Interestingly, in this remote and secluded village, two more Down syndrome children were born - a girl to a physiotherapist, and a boy to a marketing manager. All three were treated as similar identities because of their condition, but how wrong this attitude was! Each was an individual in its own right and how different from one another!

Kneesworth House Hospital

After a while, I managed to recover from all the storms and tribulations thrown my way by fate and started to think about finding a part-time job in my profession.

The chances of finding one in the immediate vicinity seemed unrealistic but life is like a box of chocolates - you never know what you are going to get! And I got a special one just round the corner from the village, in a beautiful Georgian house surrounded by extensive parkland. The hall was used for decades as a correction centre for young delinquents with high IQ, but it became "the baby" of a delightful psychiatrist, Dr Comish, who had his eye on establishing a psychiatric unit with many rehabilitation possibilities and sports facilities to enhance patients' recovery from mental disorders.

We met by chance as we drove through the grounds inspecting the place. Dr Comish welcomed us and invited us to join him on a sightseeing tour - and a very educational tour it was ... I offered my services as a part-time speech therapist and bid him goodbye. Four months later I received a letter inviting me to join the staff of the 33-bed hospital - things could not be better.

What a fantastic possibility for professional development! All kinds of people with all kinds of communication problems and difficulties - the good, the bad, and the ugly ...

And what a lesson in life! It can happen to anyone! And for many reasons!

The medium security hospital grew steadily, and at my departure, 17 years later, it contained 150 beds. The cross-section of patients was amazing and each of them was a separate case study. After a while, I decided to do some research in this new field of communication disorders in psychiatry. Having been accepted on a Master of Science Course at the University of London neuroscience department, I endeavoured to finish the part-time course in two years. I had full staff support as I was allowed to use my patients' progress data with their permission. The results were discussed with my supervisor in London once a week and the presentation of 30,000 words of my findings was to be published in a folder form. It was an experience in itself as I had to confront the statistic, graphic and systemic issues.

The work was done, and we were invited to the Royal Albert Hall to receive our certificates and experience a new membership in academia. The whole tradition of wearing a special gown with a white rim to indicate the type of degree, curtsying in front of Princess Anne, the University Patron at the time, in full regalia, and soaking up this historic event in the middle of London was unforgettable ... and the fact that I was the only Pole with such distinction made me really proud.

My Third Daughter Joins The Clan...

Sophie came two weeks late - a little, inquisitive bundle of joy, who took time to arrive and face the world! She was a good baby, but terribly unhappy in the cold. Bath times were the most challenging, and it took her a long while to get used to them. But she achieved her developmental milestones as per expectations and travelled with us everywhere we went, starting with her first visit to Poland. The novelty of the place interested her and she was very receptive to the members of the family, be it in Warsaw, Silesia or in the Lake District. We enjoyed the trips and the food - a real treat for us at that time. My parents visited us regularly and their presence had a very positive influence on the girls' development... even when the crisis struck.

Moving to Litlington

My then-husband decided to build a new family house, and the whole project failed abominably because of various factors. The end result was that I and the children became homeless, losing our home and the newly- built house to the bank. We had to move to temporary council accommodation in a nearby village and leave Bassingbourn. Their ruthless repossession disregarding our plight was hurtful... Ken was left to his own devices. After the move and the divorce, our life continued happily in a bungalow in a quiet, classic English village famed for the discovery of an ancient Roman villa from about the second century AD, with its 30 rooms and an adjacent cemetery, and first references to it in the Domesday Book in 1242.

The girls were growing quickly. Caroline passed the entrance exam to the private St. Mary's School in Cambridge and was granted a bursary. Emma continued at her primary school in Bassingbourn with a delightful helper who stayed with her throughout her school years. Sophie - my Sunshine Slavonic blondie with blue eyes - was mostly placed with a local childminder when I worked and went to the nursery a couple of mornings a week.

I felt great - even though I had to act as if everything under the sun was great. The most challenging was taxiing the girls to three schools in three places, but we managed well with a helping hand from other parents, by sharing the lifts. Our life became very organised and full of after-school activities.

All of them were keen dancers so ballet, jazz and modern sessions were on the cards. That and the piano lessons, gymnastic hours, horse riding sessions, birthday parties, outings and travels kept us busy.

Holidays With My Treasures

We went mostly on package holidays to the Spanish Balearic Islands and Tunisia. Mallorca was very attractive with its mild climate, beaches, local entertainment and lots of interesting places to visit; the capital Palma - especially the massive Gothic Cathedral and surrounds; the south Caves of Dragon, 4km-long caves full of unforgettable nature's designs and formations which the visitors are allowed to search by foot and at the end of the trek are treated to a classic live concert performed by the musicians on the lake... quite something. Not forgetting the ever-winding road Sa Calobra and Valldemossa in the west - a beautiful town hidden in the mountains, interesting not only because of its time-forgotten atmosphere but also for its famous inhabitants - Chopin and George Sand who desperately tried to nurse him back to health in this highest Mallorquin treasure.

The museum tells a heroic story of the feminist mother of two and her quest to be accepted as an unmarried mother and a lover in this traditional and very religious Spanish enclave in the mid-19th century. She wrote a book about her experiences praising the beauty of the island. but cursing the prejudiced villagers.

Our Tunisian trips happened regularly every two years for a decade: always to Skanes near Sousse - a traditional Moorish town full of action, noise and muezzins calling the faithful to their prayers five times a day! The hotel was situated right on the beach with international clientele, a children's club and a variety of evening shows. During the day we had a chance to explore Tunis and its famous Bardo museum with its exquisite collection of Roman mosaics; or visit a beautiful Sidi Bou Said village overlooking a bay with its characteristic white and blue houses and where the Arab Spring started in 2011, when a local businessman set himself on fire in protest against the regime; or travel to El Jem - the best preserved Roman amphitheatre in the world, or even still venture south to the Sahara desert to admire Matmata, full of Berber cave houses and some Star Wars filming sites.

On quieter days we enjoyed the beach and its attractions - the speedboats, the pirate ships, the pedaloes, and my favourite ever: paragliding off the beach! The silence up there beats everything - the best therapy nature can offer! Either alone or in tandem with Emma, we glided under the parachute, stunned by the views around us. Unforgettable moments ... and unforgettable emotions ...

And on Sundays, we joined the international Catholic congregation at the local church of St. Felix, conducting the masses in five languages: English, Spanish, French, German and - much to my surprise - Polish with full involvement of the visitors. Excellent idea for international unification ...

And every year, we went to Poland, be it Warsaw, Cracow, with its unique positive energy and treasures in the Old Square, the salt mine in Wieliczka and the infamous Auschwitz concentration camp or picturesque Zakopane in the Carpathian Mountains - a paradise for hikers, skiers, or those who prefer lazing about in these spectacular high mountains.

Warsaw was the closest to my heart as I was born and lived there for 22 years. The defiant town with brave history and risen from the 95per cent dead after the maniacal Nazis persistently bombed it during WW2. It is beautifully located with the Vistula River parting the place into two sections - all full of greenery, parks and an array of historical architectural gems.

The present from our political "friends" from the old USSR towered over the centre - the Palace of Culture and Science - impressive in its grandiosity and celebrating the socialist concept of superiority. They have seven of those in Moscow, and felt the need to share the monstrosity with us ... Fortunately the obsession to keep up with the West is still alive, and the Manhattan-like structures - although totally out of Warsaw character - help to conceal this symbol of Russian dominance over 40 post-war years.

The Lazienki (bathrooms) Park is an escape to serenity, with its unique positive energy, its undulating terrain, the Royal Palace overlooking the lake, and an adjacent amphitheatre still used for the performances. And its summer Chopin concerts were performed by world-famous pianists under Chopin's monument in the rose garden. True magic... As is the Old Town - reconstructed in full and in detail with painstaking work to bring it to its pre-war glory. The Varsovians succeeded and it is a feast - in every sense of the word - to walk its streets.

Back to Bassingbourn

After a year-and-a-half, our temporary accommodation in Litlington was exchanged for a new three-bedroomed house in Bassingbourn - we were back in the old village with all its amenities and familiarities. I still acted as a family taxi driver and breadwinner, which involved taking the girls to their respective schools: Caroline to Cambridge, Emma to the local primary, and Sophie to her first school in Royston. Some lifts were arranged with their friends' parents, so we managed well with the arrangements. The girls were bringing certificates from all possible activities making me proud and feeling positive as a single parent. We attended all shows they took part in and admired their skills. They also visited their father with mixed feelings for a while, but once they were able to decide for themselves, the visits stopped.

At some stage, I was offered an evening job in the nearby village college teaching Spanish and Polish. My linguistic vocation could develop further and make a change from the structured life we were living. We set up two groups of mixed ability. Both groups were very enthusiastic and the teaching atmosphere was very positive. We had lots of challenges facing us, considering various levels of language acquisition within the Spanish group but all was well for more than two years. In the Polish group, I had 10 beginners with various Polish connections and a common ambitious aim to learn the language. Unfortunately, we finished the course a year later with only four students - the complexity of the lingo put them off.

Whilst I was working in the evenings, the girls were looked after by many young childminders - a new type of social contact which benefited their development. We also went away to places such as Center Parcs and Pontin's where the onus of relaxation was on families, and the facilities accommodated all age groups. My parents used to join us on many occasions during their visits, and so did my nieces and my brother. Caroline moved out to Cambridge soon after we settled in the new house. She was closer to her friends and school.

Emma had to undergo some additional operations to correct new developmental cardiac issues. Sophie was growing and shining in her own special way with her inquisitive nature, and zest for trying new things bar the piano lessons - it was not her cup of tea.

CHAPTER 5

OUR LONGER
FOREIGN BREAKS

Canary Islands

Every Easter, and in half-term breaks in autumn, we travelled to warmer climates. Apart from our twice-yearly holidays in Tunisia, we had many short breaks in other parts of the world, starting with the Canary Islands, especially Tenerife. The climate was perfect for all of us, and there were lots of things to do with the major attraction being the fourth highest active volcano in the world – Mount Teide. I must admit that it was my personal favourite as I am an ardent fan of anything to do with volcanology.

Also, we enjoyed the visits to its famous Loro Parque full of interesting creatures found all over the world. The beaches are of all kinds, from sandy to black volcanic or rocky ones. The views are fantastic from land and from the sea, where one can enjoy seeing the centuries-old lava formations adorning the coast.

Another island of similar type in the archipelago is Lanzarote with its black volcanic sand everywhere, subterranean caves which served a local artist Cesar Manrique as inspiration to create a house - a perfect permanent sunscreen all year round ... Finally, Fuerteventura with its pristine sand dunes ... and many others.

Cyprus

Cyprus was very diverse not only for its political partition, but for its Roman and climatic characteristics: enjoying the beach in the morning and having a snowball fight later at the top of the island - next to the military base on Mt. Olympus. And taking up the chance to visit Egyptian and Israeli hot spots the Pyramids of Giza and Jerusalem on one-day cruises. The Great Pyramid was accessible to tourists so we walked the claustrophobic tunnel bent double to the centre. The end result was disappointing as the chamber was grey and smelly and housed only one empty sarcophagus. The walk in Jerusalem along the Via Dolorosa following the Stations of the Cross - full of noisy Arab vendors beckoning to visit their shops - was moving as much as the visit to the Holy Sepulchre church built in the fourth century over the skull-shaped hill named Golgotha - the traditional site of the crucifixion and burial of Jesus. We were allowed to touch the actual hole left in the rock by the cross - a shuddering experience.

Canada

Canada was a different venture altogether, not only because of its distance, but also a complete change in the landscape. We stayed mainly in Toronto among lakes, colourful forests and sheer natural beauty, unspoilt by human greed. That included a second wonder of the world, Niagara Falls - known from my travels before, but this time shrouded in fog and breeze especially felt on the boat "Maid of the Mist" which approaches the side of the Canadian Falls and gives the adrenaline junkies the feel of their power and might.

We also made many visits to the Spanish mainland; Barcelona, Valencia and Malaga made a permanent mark in our memories. The people, the food, the atmosphere - all at their best and welcoming ... Not to mention architectural gems near Malaga, such as old Ronda, Seville and Granada, and hyper- modern museums in Valencia. Especially its world-famous City of Art and Science which includes structural novelties, for example, a building resembling a giant eye, housing an IMAX cinema and a planetarium, an interactive museum of science, which resembles the skeleton of a whale and at its entrance, the Walk - an open structure enveloping a landscaped walk with indigenous plant species and an outdoor contemporary art gallery. Amazing place with mind-boggling constructions and experimental ventures - human imagination and determination are limitless ...

All that in addition to long, sandy beaches blue seas, mountains, caves, colourful flora and refreshing breeze ...! Gracias Espana!

Madeira

The first visit to Madeira was yet another positive memory. Stuck in the middle of the Atlantic Ocean, green and rugged with its spiky cliffs, pebbly beaches, and subtropical climate, its exclusive vegetation, wine and centuries-long customs and traditions make it a very special place.

Funchal - the capital - also offers a unique opportunity of admiring the island from the top of the hill overlooking the port: in a toboggan pushed by skilled drivers down the winding streets at your preferred speed. The views are spectacular and the fun is immense!

Cuba

Heading further west across the Pond, we enjoyed our trip to Cuba - still under the socialist rule of Castro et al, and devoted to celebrating their hero Che Guevara - the Marxist revolutionary from Argentina. Both are still the focus of life education, and reverence ... People are poor but kind and very happy with their simple life, with only the basics provided. Highly controlled and desperate for contact with the real world - so familiar to me and taking me back to my childhood.

The hotel in the eastern part of the island near Guantanamo Bay was impeccable, the beaches of fine, white sand within arm's reach and the hammocks between the palm trees. It was beautiful, warm, and relaxing ... until I fell off one of them and did a backward flip, nearly breaking my neck.

The visit to the hospital, X-ray is done with a Russian built machine resembling times before I was born and highly specialized doctors. This healing combination aided my slow recovery. And mother nature came to my rescue as well: during the swimming with dolphins' session, which I dreaded, I was advised to float in my safety jacket. Not to add insult to injury ... Suddenly, two gorgeous grey creatures swam under both of my arms and carried me across the basin - they knew I was unwell and helped me to enjoy the experience. What a treat! Both were rewarded with many strokes and kisses ...

Cruising

We also started experimenting with cruising holidays, starting with the Canary Islands and Morocco voyages. What a fantastic way to see so many spots in a week! From Spanish Grand Canaria, Tenerife, Fuerteventura to Moorish Casablanca with its typical Mauresque architecture and the second largest mosque in the world by the Atlantic Ocean - a jewel in the Moroccan artisan crown. And made famous by the film of the same title with Ingrid Bergman and Humphrey Bogart - filmed entirely in ... Hollywood!

We finished the cruise in Madeira - the revisit was worth every minute. We had a chance to relive the first encounter - and to admire new findings. The medium-size cruise ship offered luxury in every sense of the word: service, food, entertainment, and endless opportunities to meet people from every corner of the world and enjoy ourselves. We were hooked!

New Work Experiences

The hospital was expanding and new wards were being added for various mental conditions: from personality disorders, schizophrenia and learning disabilities to all kinds of unusual mental disturbance cases, including elective mutism, autism, anorexia and bulimia. There were also two bungalows in the grounds dedicated to the clients in the transitional phase on their way back into the community. After a while, the pastime opportunities included gym sessions, animal care in the mini-zoo, agricultural jobs, and a large range of educational/ therapeutic subjects.

My case load was so varied and interesting that I decided to use this unique opportunity and set up a research project for the good of science. My cases included people with communication difficulties, be it comprehension, expression or sheer interaction problems. I was involved in therapeutic programmes for people of various backgrounds and disabilities - most with forensic histories.

The most successful was the case of a young man who arrived at the hospital from London with no verbal communication at all. I offered my sessions to this apparently mute individual, and for weeks encouraged him to communicate. He responded and told me about his origins in Guyana, maternal physical abuse and his psychological problems. He was very cooperative and his treatment was his door to freedom. He left the hospital and was placed in a hostel in his familiar London area.

One day I received a phone call from a very happy young man who thanked me for my help and support and informed me that he was waiting for a council flat to start his new life. Best reward ... it took a humane approach, a positive attitude and a listening ear to change someone's life ...

There were other clients with a history of drug taking and the consequences of such life experiences, including a concert organ player who once shared a joint at a party and paid for it with developing schizophrenia. Another one was an ex-SAS team member who had schizophrenic episodes with excessive aggression, but was doing well with treatment until he had a total relapse and was transferred to a high-security hospital for the rest of his life. Another interesting case was a personality disorder victim who was a very sensitive and creative person. His forte was poem writing, and I was very honoured to be given a collection - still in my possession - to be presented at the public writers' meeting. A week later he took his life ...

Sometimes the mental confusion and helplessness of the situation led people to extreme decisions, but with timely support and competent treatment, many a life can be retracked and saved to allow them to return to, and function in, society. My research evaluated the need for speech and language therapy and included proof of its efficacy in the psychiatric hospital environment as a part of the multidisciplinary team approach in the treatment and rehabilitation of its patients.

To support them, I decided to combine the pleasant with the useful. As an avid geology fan, I embarked on a mission seemingly impossible, although probable ...

Bon Jornu, Etna!

My, yet another, once in lifetime experience started by chance. I spotted an advert for a fundraising expedition to Mt. Etna, organised by the mental health charity MIND. I had to go ... the largest and still active European volcano was beckoning ... what a treat! So after some futile attempts to gather the necessary funds from local firms - after all the subject matter is not very socially attractive - I decided to finance it myself. The hospital supported me partially and at the end of September I was off to Catania for a long weekend with a group of volcano enthusiasts.

We were allocated double bedrooms in a shelter in Piano Provenzana and introduced to the plan for the big day the next morning. The idea was to climb the volcano from 2000m as the arduous trek to the top was to take more than three hours. And then walk all the way back to the shelter.

The morning was glorious. Not a cloud in the sky, perfect air quality and the views unforgettable. We were taken by Jeeps to the snow-clad slope and started the adventure. The Lady was not impressed ... Our competitors were a French group who managed to overtake us at times, but that did not concern us - we were more attentive to the humming and gargling noises coming from underneath our feet. The Sicilian guide was smiling and kept encouraging us to continue the climb regardless. So we did and finally reached the top at 3000m - or tops as there are four summit craters - just to be shrouded by the suffocating sulphuric cloud - the Lady was not welcoming ... the guide became worried and started shouting "let's go" - but where to? Everything was foggy and confusing ...

Finally, we were guided down the hill and reached the lower levels to find the blue sky back in view. The next day was spent sightseeing in local lava caves. The whole experience was unreal! And to think that a month later Etna exploded and the lava flow reached our shelter up to four metres high ... the solid magma is still there right on the back of the building - a gruesome reminder of the charge: the Greek mythical goddess of volcano Etna.

It makes one stop and rethink one's insignificance when confronted by the powers of nature and the devastation that so-called civilized humans have inflicted upon it to their own detriment ...

More Local Discoveries

My treasures continued to surprise me: from Caroline's academic, sports and dancing achievements (she even managed to get an O level in Polish at the Polish School in Cambridge!), Emma's school progress and ever- growing collection of rosettes for her horse riding and Sophie's open and methodical approach to life. My Sweetie was making life more palatable, my Star was shining contrary to general expectations and my Sunshine was lightening our challenging days.

In time, Caroline moved from Cambridge to Leeds to study media and business with a graduation ceremony which really made me very proud of her achievement after the many hiccups and mishaps that had crossed her path. Emma moved from primary school to our local college and continued to defy the pessimists with her artwork and - much to my surprise - a certificate of outstanding work in maths! Sophie was a creative and imaginative pupil, with great gains in writing and acting. The shows we attended, and exams taken, seemed continuous. The birthday parties as well.

We also explored the surrounding villages and sea-side resorts. The most attractive for many reasons was the nearby Royal Bassingbourn Barracks, where every year the largest hangar accommodated the Glenn Miller Orchestra and hundreds of visitors dressed in WW2 clothes, commemorating the war times and the international pilot squadrons who flew from the airstrip to Europe. Glenn Miller did so as well, but never returned, reported missing in action ...

Ashwell village, with its 11 centuries of history with the source of river Cam in five freshwater springs. It hosted Romans, Vikings and Black Death and lots of mishaps, but thrived with its traditional cricket ground, amazing Tudor buildings and a collection of various old buildings, including a village lockup for drunks and suspected criminals.

The Folly in Wimpole Park - my relaxation hub

Another place worth visiting was Wimpole Park estate: a beautiful park and a neo-classical stately home with an adjacent church still housing the original organ and stained-glass windows with the impressive white, red and grey marble tombs of the local nobility. The estate is sited near the Roman Road leading straight up to Scotland, and was first noted in the Domesday Book of 1086.

Queen Victoria and Prince Albert visited the house in 1843, dined and attended the ball in their honour. Now under the auspices of the National Trust, its last owner was Rudyard Kipling's daughter Elsie. The north woodland is guarding the Folly - a false Gothic tower overlooking the lakes and the Hall with its Dutch gardens. The place is charming, historic and full of positive energy.

Travelling east, we came across another stately jewel Audley End, near Saffron Walden. One of the finest Jacobean houses, renowned for its palatial architecture and its use during WW2 by the Special Operations Executive. It was a training ground for the 600 Cichociemni (the Silent Unseen - the elite special operations paratroopers of the Polish Army in exile, to operate in occupied Poland), who are remembered with the monument by the entrance dedicated to 108 of them who died in action.

My Individual Adventures

Every year my birthday was a special treat. As a keen follower of Formula 1, I was given a ticket to drive a Ferrari in a training circle at Silverstone. Another time my gift was a ride across London on a Harley Davidson with a leather-clad driver - a true biker who suggested we start at the Hard Rock Cafe near Park Lane and go all the way to Richmond Park to enjoy nature at its best in the autumn. My tandem sky-dive for Great Ormond Street Hospital - a little thank you for saving Emma - was an exhilarating experience, with an unexpected dive through the clouds - damp and cold but groovy!

Every year I had an opportunity to travel anywhere I wanted and a chance to see things I was interested in. The first trip took me on the Nile cruise from Luxor to Aswan, stopping every day at a different temple marvel of human potential: from Luxor's Karnak and Luxor temples to Hatshepsut, Kom Ombo and Philae giants - all impressively enormous and distinctly different. What a lesson in the history of the Father of African Rivers decorated here and there with large wooden sailing boats called feluccas. The luxury of the cruise ship, food, interesting company and unforgettable views were an addition to the relaxing treat and a promise to bring the girls to see it all one day ...

Sicily was another feat. I fell in love with the island, its sweet lemons, tranquillity and zest for life, despite the active volcano, which is renowned for its unexpected strombolic activity. I was hoping for some spectacular fireworks displays, but instead, I had a chance to see the place totally covered in brown ash due to the volcanic activity overnight - the lava rain. Brilliant fertilizer but a pain to clear ... Still, all are so respectful of Mt. Etna and used to her unpredictable excesses that it is no bother to the Sicilians ... they continue with their traditions and accept her reign.

Scuba diving in Hurghada in Egypt was a sporty event full of preparations, instructions and safety gear. We were taken to a swimming pool initially to familiarize ourselves with the equipment and the rules. The next day was more challenging as we went out on the Red Sea and were expected to try diving with a buddy. Face to face with starfish, moray eels, and masses of colourful shoals passing by. Quite an undersea thrill if it was not for the decline in the coral reef tracts through pollution and climate change. My buoyancy was also faltering because of a stinking cold, but on the whole another interesting encounter with nature.

Another volcanic happening was on the Aeolian Island of Stromboli - located north of Sicily, and called the lighthouse of the Mediterranean - with its ever-active volcano showing off its regular strombolic eruptions at the summit with lava, volcanic bombs and pyroclastics. And only 500 inhabitants. The nearby quaint Strombolicchio - a basalt rock - is a remnant of the collapsed volcano declared a nature reserve for its unique flora and fauna.

And not forgetting my tour across northern Europe as a trainee for an exclusive group travel company, which aimed at establishing travel by train only. Each participant was expected to prepare a guiding tour in each port of call - a challenge everyone had to face to pass the guiding test.

We started in Finland on a grey day in Helsinki. The capital is famous for its diverse architecture and Nordic cuisine. We only had time to visit the Square and the adjacent streets overlooking the Baltic Sea. The next day was a ferry day, taking us across the strait to Tallin - the capital of Estonia. This picturesque place with the cobbled Old Town and many buildings from centuries ago welcomed us with sunshine... The terracotta roofs and white walls produced an unusual view, with the 13th century 64m church tower rising in the middle of the old quarter.

From there we travelled to Latvia and its capital Riga, a cultural centre with many brick and wooden buildings and a fantastic open-air museum of wooden sculptures.

The next stop was in Vilnius in Lithuania, a beautifully restored old town with rare examples of all architectural styles and cobbled streets. And it was my turn to guide the group and be as informative as possible, yet remembering not to make it boring ...

Prague in the Czech Republic was next. The city of the hundred spires with its colourful baroque buildings, gothic churches, and the animated display of the medieval Astronomical Clock chiming on the hour, much to the delight of masses of tourists. The beer bikes were everywhere offering a pedal-powered roving tour: the local beer and the pop tunes while cruising over the Vltava river with its

18 bridges - the Charles Bridge being the 15th-century construction lined with the imposing statues of the Catholic saints.

Next was Warsaw - a chance to pop round to visit the family and one or two of the beauty spots in the centre, especially the Old Town and the University. Our final stop was in Berlin: the city of progress and extravaganza ... Quite an adventure in the company of future guides - but not practical for me. The attraction was muted by the salary ... Not in my bracket of expectations. And too demanding timewise... the girls always came first.

I was also registered with casting agencies and was involved in making TV and feature films in the south of England which included the series "Call the Midwife" and "Silent Witness"; "Anna Karenina" with Keira Knightley and "Paddington" were filmed in the historic halls, adding ambience to the filming session - interesting but very demanding time-wise and travel wise...

My political involvement with the Liberal Democrats took me to the Houses of Parliament and the European Parliament as an observer. It was very short-lived. The bureaucratic establishments led by intrigue, inter- political struggles, and personal interests put me completely off the scene... Especially not doing what is being preached in the pseudo-interest of the strife of the people.

CHAPTER 6

MOVING TO ROYSTON...
ON THE PRIME MERIDIAN...

The Roysia Stone dating back to the Ice Age, and giving the name to the town.

Our Royston Jolly Postie, food and drink hub named after the old post office.

...also known as the Greenwich Meridian: the imaginary line dividing the Western hemisphere from the Eastern one - how symbolic of my coupled life!

The family was growing and spreading its wings in different directions.

After graduating from Leeds University with a degree in Business Studies and Media, Caroline was getting ready to travel with her boyfriend to live in Thailand. Emma received a GCSE certificate in art from Bassingbourn Village College and joined the art unit for special needs students at Cambridge Regional College. Sophie started the John Henry Newman secondary school in Stevenage.

The need for coordination was necessary, so I decided that the move to Royston would be the best option. The house could be rented, and we three could live in a flat in a building by the main road five minutes from the rail station - an essential asset in my view, as it gave me direct access to London in 40 minutes - and a short distance from the nearest supermarket - all basic needs on hand.

So we moved to this traditionally English small medieval town - first recorded in the old archives in 1262 - full of fascinating history. The name derives from the ice-age stone still present by the main road which is an old Roman way to Scotland. The legend has it that a Lady Roysia placed a cross in it - the indentation is still visible - hence the Roysia Stone and gave the town its name. The Priory was built by the Augustinian monks in the 1100s, and Royston became a trading centre. King James I used to come here regularly to hunt in the nearby woods. But the piece de resistance is the Royston Cave probably dug out in neolithic times, some 3000 years BC, for flint to make axes. The wall decorations of carved religious figures of St. Katherine, St. Christopher and St. George were done in the times of the Crusades, and the cave was probably used as a chapel. It was filled in about 1540, at the time of the Reformation, when King Henry VIII closed churches and monasteries. It was discovered in 1742, and is currently open to tourists on a very limited basis.

Emma was taken to Cambridge by taxi, Sophie's school bus stopped every day at the bus stop outside my window and I had a five-minute drive to work.

My family visited us for years every summer: two young nieces and my brother. They were great company for my two ladies, and even joined them at school - much to the delight of the teachers - a novelty for both sides.

We spent after-school time walking, horse-riding and visiting the interesting places in the vicinity and further afield. They included the very important holiday camps at Center Parcs and Pontin's in Pakefield - the family-orientated holiday centres which offered different levels of activities for all generations.

The first one is situated in Thetford Forest - a 40-minute drive from home, and located between Suffolk and Norfolk, known to be the largest pine forest in the English lowlands, and a paradise for mushroom pickers at the end of summer.

The Polish community in Cambridge used to organise outings for seniors - the specialists in mushroom recognition - who would descend upon the unsuspecting beauty spots to disturb their eco-system and harvest the wild delicacies found in the leaf litter. The expeditions were very popular and people used to arrive by the coachful to enjoy this unique opportunity each year and pick some porcini mushrooms, slippery jacks, chanterelle mushrooms and many other varieties available straight from Mother Nature for a very short period of time. They could be dried and used in endless recipes, pickled and eaten as a condiment to food, or simply fried and eaten as one wished. The tastes are exquisite!

The Center Parcs complex in the healthy pine forest, its modern and fully furnished bungalows scattered all over the place, the attractive landscaped lakes and forest walk trails together with the swimming pool complex and its amenities, were a great escape from the demands of an everyday organized lifestyle.

Pontin's resort was different: situated on the Suffolk coast, overlooking the North Sea and full of family attractions for all ages. There were some daily activities scheduled every day, and there was a possibility to leave the children in a highly supervised group with the leader involving them in all kinds of creative tasks. A real breather for the parents who could enjoy their time in peace and without interruptions.

Even a walk along the sandy and badly eroded beach - the sea takes a two- metre chunk of land a year - was a true treat... The town itself - Pakefield - is considered one of the earliest areas of human habitation in the UK - a mere 700,000 years ago judging by the findings in the cliffs.

It was mentioned in the first manuscript record of England and Wales, the Domesday Book, completed in 1086 as ordered by the king William the Conqueror. Currently, it is famous for its fishing industry, and its lighthouse is still in use and much appreciated by Coastwatch.

... and Venturing Much Further Afield To Asia.

This time for a family reunion in Thailand. Since Caroline and her boyfriend had left England, she was very happy and resourceful, enjoying her basic life on the island of KoPhaNgan; living in a locally constructed hut and appreciating the peaceful surroundings with very few and infrequent tourists passing the beach she stayed on. But she missed the family contact, so we decided to visit my first born and their big sister.

The island is situated in the Thai Gulf, one hour's flight south from Bangkok.

To make the journey less strenuous, the stopover was to be Abu Dhabi - the capital of the United Arab Emirates and one of the richest cities in the world. We flew Etihad Airways with its impeccable service and arrived at Abu Dhabi airport on time in the evening, went through the very efficient passport control and were met by the hotel taxi. On stepping outside the air-conditioned building into the open air, we got a shock: the heat was unbearable with a high level of humidity and Emma's glasses steamed up completely! Plus, the girls saw many women clad in their niqabs for the first time, which was a totally new experience for them. But the worst came the next , when after a generous breakfast, we decided to explore the place.

The streets were empty! The sun was beaming relentlessly on us while we walked for more than an hour in the direction of a fountain. By the time we reached the place, we were exhausted and dazed... where are the people? And where are we?

We soaked our feet in the fountain and walked back to the hotel, stopping at the only shop open to get some water... lost tourists without any idea of the local climate and traditions. The owner explained that everybody was hiding in an air-conditioned mall and no locals could be seen as nobody even poked their nose out in this heat. The masses surged outside in the evening to enjoy the cool of the Empty Quarter desert, named so by the Bedouins because of its vast and mysterious wilderness - a part of the Arabian Peninsula - the largest sand desert in the world.

We decided to join them, indirectly, in tasting the desert experience. One was the desert safari - or rather a roller-coaster ride - in a 4x4 Jeep, which was a dare-devil experience of dune bashing. The driver seemed to have forgotten about the gravity laws and was meandering in the deep sand at 45 degrees slant - my heart was pumping at double rate and all three of us were petrified of the driver's bravado. His tricks were impressive but we were left shaken and stirred. No wonder they call themselves the Desert Cowboys! Others chose quad bikes and sand boards to ride the dunes - whatever adrenaline shot you chose; the views and nature's stillness were overwhelming. The place had its specific charm and an air of mystery - Aladdin's story sprang to mind ...

The Bedouins evening was a lavish feast under the stars with delicacies, belly dancers, shisha smoking and star gazing ... talking romantic! The only attraction we skipped was the falconry show: the human-bird relationship presentation famed by the 4000 year-old tradition in the Arab countries. We returned to the hotel exhausted, had a quick dip in the roof swimming pool and collapsed, dreaming about Arabian nights ...

The next day we transferred by the local airline to Koh Samui - the second- largest Thai island famous for its palm-fringed beaches, coconut groves and dense mountainous rainforest. From there we took a ferry to our final destination.

KoPhaNgan island is located 12km from Koh Samui and is made of granite. It is famous for its unspoilt beauty, lush interior tropical jungle and long, white sand beaches, with more than 20 diving sites. From the Thongsala port we used the traditional means of transport, a tuk-tuk, which took us to the north of the island to Thong Noi Pan beach.

The place was awesome: the traditional bamboo bungalows had basic bedrooms with concrete floors, wooden beds with mosquito nets, and a very simple bathroom with a bucket serving as a shower when you pulled the cord attached to it. The whole complex was right on the beach.

The granite tables in the sand were a perfect location for a healthy breakfast, mainly consisting of the now-called thick smoothies made from local guavas, dragon fruit, rambutan, mango, papaya and pineapples - health benefits galore! Sold everywhere, ready cut and peeled as well - an exotic daily feast ... and that straight and ripened on the plant or tree. All that while overlooking the sandy stretch of the beach and the bay marked clearly by the elephant rock on one curve and the hilly formation on the other, where they built a posh hotel with amazing views over the sea. There was also a permanent feature waiting for the tourists in the sea: a Thai- specific long-tail boat moored on the beach ... available to explore this unspoilt and beautiful coastline.

We were in paradise! Simple life, no crowds, and healthy food from many restaurants of various standards inland; our favourites were the two: Handsome Burgers - a healthy type of local McDonald's - Emma's and Sophie's favourite - and Rasta Baby - my favourite with everything cool and Caribbean: from the laid-back atmosphere thanks to Bob Marley's music to delicious food concoctions such as jerk chicken and fried plantins. For more discerning clientele there was a modern new oval restaurant called Kun's, owned by aThai English couple serving more traditional examples of both cuisines.

We had such an exciting time there from fishing and snorkelling among tropical species to exploring the island and visiting the touristy places such as the elephant sanctuary, and being given a chance to see the jungle from the fairly comfortable seats attached to their backs. Another attraction was the visit to Than Sadet or Than Prawet waterfalls, which required a bit of hiking in the jungle - very refreshing tet-a-tete with Mother Nature in her ever-refreshing pristine waters ...

Shopping was done locally or by the main means of transport - the motorbike. The road left a lot to be desired, thanks to the annual monsoons ripping the road repairs on a regular basis. Bumpy but relaxed, no rush and no things to do. Fantastic mental and body therapy... Not forgetting the famous Thai massage - available both on the beach and in the parlours - the body being subjected to half-an-hour of continuous muscle pressure, which left me feeling as if I was run over by a steam roller - sore, but the next day feeling 20 years younger!

Another way to explore the surrounds was to walk from one beach to another beach. We did and decided that ours was the best for its beauty and serenity ... and the sea so blue and shallow inviting us with its constant wave murmur ... Bliss!

So, when it came to bidding goodbye I promised to return to it to repeat the healing therapy session! And I did some years later.

CHAPTER 7

BACK HOME TO...
A CREATIVE EPISODE

Emma's oil paintings "Scraping" and "A lady dancing in a Sari" exhibited in Tate Modern, London.

Emma with some of her pieces of art.

...with a bump. The change was too drastic: the climate, the air, the food and the exotic lifestyle overwhelmed us. Returning to reality was long and difficult: the daily routine and obligations seemed to have wiped out the trip benefits very quickly, but the memories and the pictures remained ... Emma's favourite hobby is reliving the experiences via her enormous collection of holiday pictures and it helps to remember the happy moments - she has become an expert in filling in details from our voyages.

School and work continued and the girls returned to their respective colleges. Sophie went to the John Henry Secondary in Stevenage, then to North Herts College to try Media Studies, which took her to Northampton University. After a year of minimal education, she decided to re-direct her interest and did a full-time nursing course at Anglia Ruskin University in Cambridge. She also learned to drive, much to her own surprise. Emma continued her art course at Cambridge Regional College and did art sessions at the Rowan Foundation studio. In addition, she volunteered at a local nursery, and both sides were delighted: the kids loved her and vice versa, much to the staff's delight.

Her GCSE in Art was well deserved, and her works caught the attention of one of the artist tutors. She submitted some of Emma's paintings to the Tate Modern Exhibition for special needs artists and - lo and behold - one of Emma's was selected to be included in the public display. We could not believe it! Emma was very excited, and so was I - my so-called disabled daughter, commonly ostracized by society, reached the artistic heights not many manage to reach! What an achievement! We were as proud as peahens! The actual visit to the exhibition was very emotional. We were sitting in the first-floor gallery overlooking Christopher Wren's biggest artwork,

St. Paul's Cathedral, and staring at the paintings with her name and title attached to them... unbelievable ... This unique happening gave me goose pimples. My brain could not register the enormity of the event in our lives.

The accolades continued when Emma was invited to exhibit her works in a London gallery called the Foundry - the written comments in the guest book were so uplifting! Then followed an interview with the artists' circle on a local London radio station - a very challenging and stressful event for Emma, but she coped.

Next came the unexpected recognition of her devotion to her work in the new studio called Rowan in Cambridge. She joined it 12 years ago and initially tried clay and woodwork sessions. Someone took a picture of her at work in the wood department polishing her wood creation - she seems to be putting her heart and soul into the process... This artist's at-work portrait won second prize in the Camden Galleries. The prizes were given to the winners by the actors from Emma's favourite TV soap EastEnders and especially John Altman and Natalie Cassidy ... who made her day! A three-fold treat!

And soon, we were enjoying yet another public display of Emma's life. This time in Leicester Square. Emma has been an ardent fan of the heavy metal band Aerosmith since her childhood, and secretly fancied the lead singer Steven Tyler. When the band visited England for the first time, we went to the Hyde Park Calling festival and spent the whole two hours in the pouring rain - she was elated and danced all the way through the gig. I took a picture of her in ecstasy, and it won the Snap competition in London. Her hair was dripping, and she was soaked, but the expression on her face said it all - she was in heaven! The winning pictures were enlarged and put on giant cubes with appropriate descriptions. The cubes were displayed in Leicester Square for a few weeks and then travelled all over England, spreading the word about the life successes of people abled differently...

Aerosmith rocks!
by Emma Anderson

The photo was taken during the Hyde Park Calling concert featuring my favourite group of all the decades, Aerosmith. I danced for two hours in the pouring rain and will never forget this fantastic experience!

CHAPTER 8

DEVELOPING A TASTE FOR LUXURY TRAVEL IN THE NORTHERN HEMISPHERE

Tendering in the Pacific

Cruising in Montenegro

Docking in British Colombia

With time we spread our travelling wings. Cruises were captivating, offered many stop-overs, and really provided a wider picture of the visited places ,with the daily trips organised in advance, and a varied, multichoice entertainment to enjoy during the day and/or to finish the day. Also, the variety of cuisines offered by many restaurants, from the self-service buffets to the waiter service ones. And last - but not least - the range of sports facilities. All on one boat sailing gracefully through the seas and spreading the tourists' horizons literally and figuratively. In essence: one big adventure in many places whilst following unknown routes in the cosmopolitan company of fellow travellers, crew, and hospitality staff, and all that in beautiful decor, cabins and style. Not to be missed ...

The Canaries

The Canary Islands cruise was our first family cruise and great fun. We sailed from Las Palmas in Grand Canaria - famous for the black lava and sand beaches to Tenerife - the largest and tallest in the archipelago, Lanzarote - mostly flat and full of quirky lava constructions, caves and volcanic landscapes, Casablanca - of "here's looking at you kid" fame thanks to Humphrey Bogart and Ingrid Bergman in the film Casablanca - a very colourful and elegant place, and finishing in Madeira - the autonomous island of Portugal, volcanic in origin, bathed in sunshine, greenery and wine.

From pebbly beaches, hilly rugged terrains, and fascinating flora, to an exclusive attraction such as the toboggan ride from the top of the hill in the capital Funchal, right down to the port, at speeds evoking screams of fear and delight! The New Year's firework display is also world-famous.

Norway Via Faroe Islands and Iceland

The contrast with the next cruise to the Norwegian fjords was staggering. We sailed from Southampton to the Faroe Islands - part of the Kingdom of Denmark, located in the Atlantic Ocean between Iceland and Norway - in cold wind, fog, and not being able to see much.

On arrival, we were welcomed by grassy heathlands, steep cliffs, and masses of seabirds, including flocks of Atlantic puffins - included as delicacies in the local cuisine. The 18 rocky islands are connected by underground tunnels, bridges, and multiple ferry routes. Torshavn - the capital - has a subpolar oceanic climate, and its main attraction is the turf- roofed houses in the Tinganes district, where the Viking parliament met for the first time in 825. And to think there are only 50,000 inhabitants living there, with the largest ethnic group being from ... the Philippines!

The next stop was geologically fascinating: Iceland - the land of Ice and Fire lying on the constantly active geological border between North America and Europe. Its Nordic architecture, dramatic volcanoes, geysers, steaming Blue Lagoon, and other steamy springs and lava spots are dotted all over this sparsely populated island, and endless waterfalls leave a permanent impression. Spectacular, wild and scary!

The next two days were spent at sea, and this gave us an opportunity to explore the treats on board: the theatre, the cinema, the disco, the jazz bar, the top deck drinks bar, and the starry skies ... spoilt for choice and new experiences.

We docked in Bergen - or rather Bryygen - and booked a local Cessna flight to take us over the famous glaciers. What a disappointment - no glacier tongues, some snow patches here and there, but the views - spectacular! Nestled in beautiful surroundings, the place is very colourful and picturesque, with wooden houses adorning the estuary of the longest and deepest fjord. Historically, it was a centre of the Hanseatic League - the German-founded empire which ruled the Baltic trading waves in northern Europe for three centuries. It was also the birthplace of Edvard Grieg - the most famous Norwegian composer.

Flam was the next stop. The village receives about 160 cruise ships per year - a great boost to the economy, but a disastrous impact on the pristine nature. It was a misty, wet, and slippery day. The village is located between two great mountains, and the local Flamsbana steam railway took us up one of the steepest trails in the world to admire hundreds of waterfalls and spectacular views. What a true nature show!

And then it was plain sea sailing - all the way home ...

USA and Mexico

We needed to warm up after the Norwegian adventure. USA and Mexico were the best options, with guaranteed warmth and sunshine. We flew to Los Angeles, California, and stayed there for a couple of days just to stretch our legs after a 12-hour flight. The modern entertainment system on the plane allows the selection of any type of visual or auditory programme, and time passes by very quickly ... On arrival, we were transported to our hotel, and my personal trip down memory lane started.

After more than 30 years I revisited local attractions, such as Hollywood and Sunset Boulevard, with a tour round the celebrity quarters in Beverly Hills, coming to the simple conclusion that the more you have, the more you spend on guarding it! And the sizes of the mansions are mind- boggling...

Then obligatory Universal Studios, with its specific displays of Hitchcock's special effects used in his thrillers, the encounter with the great white in the Jaws enclosure, the Earthquake experience of the San Francisco disaster in 1906, which left us shaken but not stirred. This was followed by extensive walks in the city passing by the Walt Disney Concert Hall in its wavy metal to the very cradle of modern LA, the pueblo of Our Lady of the Angels - named so by the Spanish settlers. Presently a very Hispanic quarter with all Mexican and full of colour.

The cruiser was awaiting us in Long Beach right next to Queen Mary in its dry dock - the most haunted attraction in America - a luxury hotel full of paranormal experiences, and available to the brave adrenaline junkies looking for ghostly fixes.

From sunny California, we sailed peacefully along the Baja Peninsula to its tip, Los Cabos. I felt so excited as two-thirds down the route, we passed the region where we lived on the Santispac beach near Mulege almost three decades before! The memories came flooding back...

We reached our destination port of El Cabo de San Lucas at sunset. The harbour was too shallow for the cruisers to dock so the tenders took us to the harbour and we watched the fishing boats coming back to the port from their Pacific Ocean conquests with their varied trophies: the enormous marlins, squids and masses of fish I have never heard of ... they needed to be cleaned and prepared for sale.

The off-cuts were thrown in heaps to the flocks of pelicans. The noise and war-like grunts took over the harbour - the fight was on and till the end! I just stood there with my camera, snatching pictures left, right and centre - nature at its best in its plight for survival.

From there, we sailed to Mexico and the first port of call, Mazatlan, nicknamed the Pacific Pearl, a thriving seaport and art centre. Set up by Spanish and German settlers at the expense of the indigenous tribe of dominating Totorames, it offers a cosmopolitan ambience and a new music genre, banda - an alteration of Bavarian folk music. Cliff jumping is also popular here - the higher the better for tips from onlooking tourists.

Puerto Vallarta was the second treat: climate, sandy beaches, promenades and nightlife at its best, with famous precious metals and stones mining industry and rich cultural heritage, made famous by Elizabeth Taylor and Richard Burton in the Night of the Iguana film in 1963. We visited the inland farms and a tequila brewery, watching the full process of extracting juice from the agave cactus - tasting included! On the way back to the cruiser, we passed bat trees full of roosting creatures and looking very ominous ...

The adventure came to an end in San Francisco, where we stayed for a couple of days to recoup our strength before flying back home.

We loved the place: undulating all the way to the Bay overlooking the Alcatraz Federal Penitentiary prison and the majesty of the Golden Gate Bridge - a glorious spectacle in both full sunshine and on a foggy day, full of every nation representative under the sun and interesting architectural gems.

Climbing steep hills by foot or by cable cars, walking the Fisherman's Wharf walk and listening to the arguing seals fighting over a spot of wooden decks floating secured off the shore ... the possibilities are endless, and with frequent climatic changes during the day, it always looks different! The views from the GGB are awesome, and strolling along the longest suspension bridge in the world, painted in its specific shade of international orange, and joining San Fran with the Pacific Ocean is a unique affair ...

Alaska

In contrast, the visit to Alaska brought our temperature down, and the landscape change was dramatic. We sailed from Seattle, the Emerald City surrounded by water, lush forests, mountains and the centre of the tech industry, home to Amazon and Microsoft, overlooked by its iconic landmark the futuristic Space Needle.

On our visit to Pike Place Market, we were treated to flowers galore, endless seafood stalls and traders tossing crabs to each other, instead of packing them as usual, to attract the tourists' attention. And Chihuly Garden with its giant glass sculptures, was a true novelty, as was the Museum of Pop Culture (named so by Jimi Hendrix) with its corrugated exterior metal structure - 3000 panels of stainless steel and aluminium shaped to reflect the ever-changing light - like music and culture which are constantly evolving ...

We sailed towards Alaska - the 49th state with 600 dramatic glaciers and three million lakes - from Elliott Bay in Seattle harbour to the Inside Passage - coastal route 52 weaving through the fjordlands of North America. Breath-taking views, total silence and natural ambience for two solid days, moving slowly towards Ketchikan. This salmon capital of the world and a paradise for totem pole lovers is humid, misty and very rainy all year round.

Surrounded by thick forests, it relies on tourism and the lumber industry. The next stop was in Juneau - the city of Alaska because of its extremely rugged terrain - the city is de facto the island city. The gold mining fame still persists and tourists can enjoy skiing, ice skating, rollerblading and many other sports depending on the season. Isolated, relaxed, totally dependent on mother nature ... Very calm, accessible only by water or seaplanes.

Skagway - made famous by John Wayne in "North to Alaska" was our last stop. The past gold rush mementoes are still visible and in summer, the local railway takes tourists over the White Pass to the place of hell - the term used to describe the then-lawless settlement full of prospectors, crooks and hopefuls.

As we walked along the pier, we saw a mountain range towering over the Yukon River and decided to go for a uniquely local experience: the husky drive - no, not in the sledges - there was no snow on the roads - but in buggies pulled by the beauties! Those Inuit-raised racers are famous for speed and resilience. They test their skills in annual sledge-dog racing and as adventure trekking dogs in winter. After the visit to the husky kennels and encounter with the newly born puppies, we had a chance to see - and feel it - for ourselves! They do run! And how!!!

We turned round and headed south. Our Alaskan trip finished in Victoria, British Colombia, on Vancouver Island. Also known as the City of Gardens – as it enjoys a temperate climate - it is located off Canada's Pacific coast and is considered to be one of the best places to live in Canada. What a tranquil, time-forgotten place. The sun was setting, cabin lights were reflecting in the sea, and the sailing and motorboats were gently rocking in one of the most beautiful harbours in the world. We were walking in this enchanted place, admiring gulls and oystercatchers, flora and the architectural remnants of Victorian colonial times. Past the Empress hotel, where king George VI and Queen Elizabeth dined during their visit and, Shirley Temple stayed with her parents ,escaping kidnapping threats made in California. Then we looked at a collection of colourful houseboats in Fisherman's Wharf and many yellow taxi boats waiting on water. The visit was short but really memorable ... in the twilight ...

Across The States

Next stop: Seattle and boarding the Amtrak train Empire Builder: the journey's last stage of 46 hours, all the way to Chicago. It was a sleeper with a glasstop carriage in the middle, allowing us to admire the eight states it runs through, especially the Rockies, the glaciers, the Mississippi river, and many stops in historically important places.

We arrived in Chicago, stayed there for a couple of days, and then returned back home to reality - full of new experiential input into our travelling experiences...

CHAPTER 9

BACK TO REALITY...

Caroline on Thong Nai Pan Noi beach, Thailand

Sophie's Triumph

The Dive to Remember!

H ome again, and everyday life brought us back to earth very quickly.

My daughters continued with their lives.

Caroline travelled in Asia and took full advantage of her freedom before returning to Cambridge. She enjoyed her Asian stretch so much that it was a painful necessity to come back to England. Her paradise spot in Ko Pha Ngan was commemorated by an unknown photographer, who took a picture of her on her own sitting on a spotless, white beach and converted it into a postcard. The place became a passing point for all the backpackers and soon became a tourist stop-over before the Full Moon Party which every year attracted thousands of young adventure-seekers, and which included drinking, taking drugs, and dancing all night ... We had a chance to join them once and decided the scene had its atmosphere but was not for us. The euphoria of the night infused with booze and dope plus the enormous noise put us off the event forever.

Caroline returned to Cambridge and started working in various jobs, including teaching English to foreign students. This new skill, which she mastered at the highest level, allowed her to travel and teach in other countries, including Spain.

Emma continued at the Rowan Foundation studio, producing ever-more interesting pieces in wood and clay, and enjoying the social aspect of attending the place. Every year in July they joined the Open Studios event in Cambridge, and the public had an opportunity to see the real pieces of art produced in different departments by students and/or supporting artists and available to buy.

We attended the studio every year and increased our art collection at home - the display shelves are full of various creations in wood, glass and clay. The word had been spreading about her achievements and many local institutions commissioned works, thus supporting this unique enterprise.

Emma also continued her horse-riding sessions which, with her trainers' support, took her to the annual Riding for Disabled competitions in Oaklands, Herts. Her collection of rosettes has been growing steadily over the years and made her proud of her great success.

Sophie moved out and bought a flat with her boyfriend Ashley. They lived nearby and maintained regular contact with us. She also loved travelling, and used to disappear from time to time to warmer climates. And it was then I had to look after Pogo - their pet tortoise which loved walking all over our flat and hiding in the most unexpected places - the most dangerous and most difficult to lift was the piano - my biceps were developing nicely...

Their engagement took place in Kenya where we went for a couple of weeks and delighted in local white sand beaches, pristine Indian Ocean waters and visiting Tsavo National Park - the largest game park in the world. The views from Voi Safari Park were as far as the horizon goes overlooking two watering holes frequented by herds of wild elephants - we could watch them for hours ...

Sophie and Ashley married in our local Catholic church. All the people present in her life managed to attend and the reception was to be in our sports centre overlooking Therfield Heath - the perfect location, with a delicious menu, space and surrounded by mother nature. They were welcomed in the centre in a traditional Polish way with a piece of bread and salt symbolizing the future wealth and life difficulties. The evening was wound up with lighting up a lantern released by the newlyweds with secret wishes up to the sky. They settled in a house in Royston - within walking distance of our flat. Sophie also decided that nursing was her career choice and switched from her Northampton media course to Cambridge.

The Anglia Ruskin University provided the necessary education, and three years later she graduated with a BSc in adult nursing. The ceremony was at the Peterborough Cathedral, where we attended with her and celebrated her great day in style. The mortarboard hats throwing concluded the ceremony and, after a short reception, we went on our way, on a grey autumn afternoon, warmed up with a champagne toast to the graduates.

I continued with my evening lessons teaching Spanish and Polish in local colleges. The Spanish group of 12 was very well matched and we stayed together for more than two years, exploring the secrets of the Hispanic culture, history and quirky language, occasionally doing the sessions in private locations.

The Polish group of 10 was also very enthusiastic and managed to stay together for nearly a year, but finished the course with only four remaining students. The reason was the complexity and pronunciation - many linguistic concepts totally unknown in English grammar and many sounds are unknown to the learners' ears. But it was a real fun challenge while it lasted!

As was my work, the whole experience of the cross-section of patients from various backgrounds, multinational staff input into improving their well-being and chances of re-joining the society formed a unique chapter in my professional life.

The initial years were very encouraging and there was a feeling of a family-like community, with the charismatic and caring, who cared about the staff as much as the patients. We felt good and appreciated on every professional level. We were all on first-name terms and participated in all events as a team.

Every Christmas, parties were organized for the children and the adults - separately. The children were treated to an entertainer and Santa with sacks of presents. The adults were enjoying the disco and symbolic gifts. Once, we were invited to a real ball in the centre of London to celebrate the anniversary of opening the KHH: tuxedos and bow ties for men, and evening dresses for ladies. Transport was provided and we were whisked away to a posh location near Hyde Park. What an experience and treat for the staff!

Guy Fawkes day on November 5 (when the Gunpowder Plot to blow up Parliament in 1605 failed) was marked with a traditional barbecue in the hospital grounds.

But as the hospital grew from 30 beds to 150, and became a money-spinner for private owners, the core idea of its founder to rehabilitate the patients to the maximum of their capabilities started to wane ... I decided that after 17 years of helping the needy it was time to leave the place, as the onus was on financial profit and not the human gain. So, I left much to my dismay that most of my efforts in many cases would not be continued as there was no replacement for the position of a communication therapist and slowly they started to close down supportive therapies, including the garden and animal enclosure which provided much-needed therapy. The teaching department had less staff and many other alternatives were abandoned. It was a pity as, with an appropriate attitude and individual approach to the patients, many of them managed to regain self-worth, improve their self- esteem and return to their social groups. Some successfully, some less so, returning to Kneesworth, or being referred to more secure institutions, which was basically the end of their rehabilitation.

Some cases ended in a drastic move of self-destruction (one of them managed to give me some heart-breaking poems to read in public when the opportunity arose), others left the establishment and re-socialized to a great effect - all with disturbing backgrounds, family histories and fears imprinted by the cruel human encounters.

There was life after Kneesworth House Hospital: I registered with the interpreting agencies and started supporting the incoming Polish and Spanish settlers who flocked into this country thanks to European Union agreements, in many ways and many places all over the country.

My personal horizons were stretching in the upward direction. I started flying lessons in the airfield on a private farm. It all began with the annual air shows organized by the owner - an avid aeroplane enthusiast and aerobatics champion, whose collection of aeroplanes was also impressive. I approached him during one of the displays and was in! From the moment I sat in a Cessna 150, I was liberated! Taking off on the bumpy field in a shaking aeroplane and staring at the orange sleeve to work out the wind direction, was only the beginning of the fantastic adventure up there!

The views, the beast and its gadgetry, the ever-changing position and manoeuvres - the adrenaline rush was exhilarating... I loved it! My total is 25 hours, which I managed to complete at the nearby Bourn airfield following the closure of the flying school half-way through my training. Bourn was a famous RAF strip built during WW2 for heavy bombers: Wellingtons, Stirlings and Lancasters. The take-off and landing conditions were smoother as the strips were covered with bitumen. All staff were old airmen with stories to tell ... Unfortunately, my dream came to an end. The place was sold to a developer and new houses are being built there ... Oh, how right Bob Dylan was: the times they are a-changing ... and my PPL license was not to be ...

But the chance to fly again came up when we agreed to do a skydive for the Great Ormond Street charity with Sophie, her ex-husband and his sister. Two nurses, an accountant, and a retired mother ... The whole action was set up to raise the money for the jump for GOSH to say thank you for their expertise in saving Emma's life - the op was so successful that she is still surprising with her strength and skills at 40!

We tried on many a Saturday to join the others in this amazing experience but English weather - as unpredictable as it is with six different weather fronts crossing over the island - was winning! Eventually, the day came when we were allowed to sky-dive with the buddy, of course. Mine was a cheerful guy dressed as a Mohican in a colourful costume - very relaxing and relieving the anticipation tension.

The plane with 20 of us took to the skies and, within minutes, we were off remembering to adopt the initial banana position with the head tilted back and feet tucked under the plane exit - as per the initial instruction prior to the flight. The wind was strong and threw us sideways and we free-fell for a while at 10 metres/second. The G forces were doing their job and we were thrust upwards with our faces contorted, and suddenly all was peaceful and gentle ... the parachute was opened and we descended quietly through the clouds looking down on the Earth and revelling in the deafening silence ... Heaven - literally! Far too short! The whole affair was over in no time ... more, please!

And there was more: we did a skydive with a solicitors firm in Cambridge in support of Emma's studio: this time, it drizzled all day and we dived through grey clouds. What an unpleasant feeling - like diving through a shower, but once we were close to landing, the views were unforgettable- once again! Feet up and we landed on our bottoms, sliding along the field and dragging the parachute behind us - a different kind of fun ...

The only similar adrenaline rush I experienced was while paragliding - but it also ended too quickly. And during my birthday Silverstone treat, when I was allowed to do laps in the Ferrari training car. Looking back, my first ride on a Harley Davidson as a teenager in Poland could match it as well; the return journey from a forest-based party back to Warsaw is still vivid in my memory ... Speed should be my middle name!

CHAPTER 10

EXPLORING THE PACIFIC REGION

The banyan (sacred tree) in La Haina, Hawaii

*Crossing the equator and kissing the fish
as a sign of respect for the Ocean*

Auckland – We Meet Again...

T he most exotic trip we have ever undertaken was the Pacific cruise which started in the Hawaiian capital Honolulu in the northern hemisphere and finished in Sydney, Australia, in the south.

Hawaii

Emma was very excited as we travelled to Los Angeles yet again, and stopped at a hotel near the LAX airport. The visit was a two-day stop-over; soon we were flying east to the Oahu island, home of the iconic Waikiki sand beach - the surfing forefather Duke Kahanamoku started the craze here - volcanic ridgelines and the Pearl Harbour naval base attacked by the Japanese Navy Air Service during WW2, when the USA was still a neutral country. Unfortunately, we arrived there in the late afternoon and did not have a chance to visit any of the places of interest.

The cruiser sailed through the night and the next day docked in La'haina. The name means a cruel sun which describes the sunny, dry climate. The place is known for its famous visitors, such as Mick Fleetwood from Fleetwood Mac, who, together with Emma's idol Steven Tyler from Aerosmith, set up an exclusive restaurant overlooking the bay, and many film-makers who chose the island to film Jaws, Jurassic Park and the Pirates of the Caribbean, among many others. There is even a bench with Forrest Gump's shoes by it and his suitcase with a box of chocolates - life-like as "you never know what you gonna get"; the sun-drenched tourist can find a shaded shelter, put his feet in Gump's shoes – literally - and contemplate.

The most famous attraction is the biggest banyan tree in the USA, planted in 1873 to commemorate 50 years of the first arrival of the American Protestant mission; spreading upwards to a height of 18 metres and rooted into 16 major trunks supported by wooden poles - they are the roots which descend from the branches and become trunks. This fig tree can provide shade for about 1000 people!

The place is full of artistic sculptures from recycled wood and sun-dried fruits, and the palm tree leaves serve as a perfect material to create all forms of animal souvenirs: mine is a fish given to me for good luck ... it is still on display on my shelf in my sitting room.

The fish is a symbol of a deeper awareness of our unconsciousness and connects us with water. There was plenty of it on the way south in many forms including a touch of typhoon risen waves. We were sailing for three days and rocked all the way to the equator. The entertainment was great, as usual, and we could search the programmes every day trying to fit in all the lectures, shows and concerts, not to mention discos.

The Equator

The crossing the equator party was exciting and, apart from endless dances, congas and champagne celebrations, it involved the kissing of the fish ritual, considered to be bringing luck to the travellers.

It was definitely true in our case: the sea calmed down and we were in the French Polynesian waters in Oceania in no time. The 130 islands are located in the South Pacific, midway between Australia and South America.

Tahiti and Bora Bora

I could feel my heart beating when we docked in Tahiti in the Papeete Harbour. I was here again after 30 years keeping my promise to Emma that one day I would take her to the places I visited on my trip round the world.

The inland trip guide was already by the coach, and we headed towards the Botanical Gardens established by H. Smith in 1920 and including magnificent specimens from Asia, Africa, Europe and Australia. The heavenly tranquil and colourful garden seemed like paradise ... with streams, brooks and waterfalls.

Next, we visited a Polynesian marae: a nearly sacred place reserved for ceremonial, social and religious ceremonies. Differing in architecture and ornaments from island to island, they reflected the societies with extremely marked hierarchies. It was a centre of political and religious games between chiefdoms. The ambience was very spiritual and respectful: meditation, rituals, the communion of specialists with the gods in prayers, chants and invocations to ancestors and divinities and sacrifices took place for centuries. Having been spiritually uplifted, we returned to the harbour and waited for the departure towards Bora Bora.

The island's name originates from the local Tahitian meaning "created by the gods." Discovered by a Dutch explorer in 1722, it is surrounded by a turquoise lagoon protected by a coral reef with fantastic scuba-diving spots with lemon shark, sea turtles and dolphins. The dormant volcano Mt. Otemanu overlooks the luxury overwater bungalow suites on stilts and beachfront villas.

Our visit was very short as we drove along the only road past lush greenery to a place of rest and a local folklore show. Everyone was relaxed and very friendly. One of the stops was near a local house and we had a chat with the family. They told us the place was very nice indeed, but boring ... So, the youngsters choose new pastures, mainly in France - the old motherland. The leaning palms with metal bands to stop the coconut crabs from climbing the trees were a novelty. The sea was pristine blue, the beach was pristine white, and the atmosphere was pristine happy ...

New Zealand

New Zealand was next. We docked in Auckland and were off as quickly as we could with our tight itinerary. It was so moving to step on the North Island soil: the memories came flooding in. The taxi took us first to the One Tree Hill area - the one and only tree was nowhere to be seen ... it was cut down times ... and the hill became home to a flock of sheep. The statistics were three million people and 10 million sheep in 1982 – some of which were crossing our path as we drove towards the house we lived in 35 years ago. The bungalow was very neglected, the veranda as well ... the only cheerful sight was a tangerine bush with some fruit ready to be picked ... just like the old times.

Then we rushed to the North Shore Hospital, where I ran a stroke group and, the nearby lake where I had spent many a lunchtime contemplating my fate and feeding black swans. We repeated the action yet again - their offspring were still graciously there.

The next stop was at Waitakere Hospital, where I ran a dementia group, and to my surprise, the place was redecorated and refurbished with the information labels printed first in Mauri and second in English. The only person I met was an elderly nurse who, to my introduction as an ex- employee, reacted "and not much has changed here, has it?" Indeed, it hasn't but the warm memories remain, and I kept my word: Emma could see the places I used to visit before she was born.

We sailed overnight from Auckland to the Bay of Plenty in the north of the North Island. It was a very sentimental departure ... wishing we could have stayed a bit longer, but the schedule was tight, and we waved goodbye to the beautifully illuminated Sky Tower and the Waitemata Harbour, passed Rangitoto Island - the only volcano which erupted from the sea - and followed eastwards.

The next morning we were off the cruiser, enjoying the landscape as James Cook did nearly 300 years ago. The only active volcano situated on White Island has a continuous eruption record of 25 years - the longest in the world. The place was very laid back and full of history as the Treaty of Waitangi was signed there in 1840 between Queen Victoria's governor and the tribes considering the Maori ownership of their lands and other properties and giving them rights of British subjects. The treaty gave the sole right to purchase the land to the British government: it is still considered the founding document of New Zealand.

Australia

Our final destination was Sydney, where we arrived early in the morning and had a chance to admire the Sydney Harbour Bridge ahead of us and the Sydney Harbour with its gem, the Sydney Opera House, from the top deck prior to disembarking. The cruise was finished and we continued our Aussie exploration for a further couple of days in Sydney, and then Cairns.

This cosmopolitan gateway to Australia is most popular for its laid-back outdoor lifestyle, vibrant nightlife and spectacular sightseeing. We started with walking the Harbour Bridge overlooking the bay and the Opera House - a design baby of a Danish architect.

The ex-warehouse renovations were full of attractive restaurants and cafes. The views over the Sydney Harbour were unforgettable: full of all kinds of sailing boats, ferries, motorboats and windsurfers painting the water white with the gracious sail-like Opera House overlooking the commotion. It was getting very hot. Looking for shade, we reached this unique architectural gem - the roofs covered with glazed ceramic and light reflecting tiles - a photographic paradise for picture taking - and available to visit inside - a true constructional wonder! Its modern expressionist design makes it one of the 20th century's most distinctive buildings. We sat on the steps watching life go by, and planning our evening as the Darling Harbour firework display was a tourist must. It was worth waiting for and enjoyed by the international crowd gathered alongside the passage dotted with restaurants and cafes offering cuisines from all over the world. Harbourside centre looked after shopping needs.

The next day was spent in the city centre and its historical quarters full of colonial remnants and restored buildings. Emma was very tired - the heat was affecting her - while I was loving the interesting facades and snapping them, she sat down on the pavement and waited patiently. On my return, I found her holding some change - a lady had given her some dollars because she thought Emma was begging! Well, she definitely earned her bottle of Coke Zero!

The visit to the Blue Mountains outside Sydney and its surrounds culminated with an Aboriginal show with indigenous poetry, singing and dancing ... Thousands of years of history accompanied by the ceremonial sounds of a didgeridoo ...

Cairns was totally different: away from the madding crowd, relaxed and in the far north, also known as a gateway to the Great Barrier Reef. The local botanical garden was a real treat for me. I found myself walking all by myself in the tropical jungle full of unusual specimens of flowers and foliage, clumps of bamboo plants covered with tourist mementoes carved on their stems. I passed a variety of unknown tropical and medicinal species of all shapes and , including a fall webworm cocoon engulfing the entire branches for the females to lay their eggs and to feed off - quite an eerie sight but with no danger of damage to the tree itself.

There were also giant flycatchers, palm trees and subtropical flowers unknown to most in the northern hemisphere. The experience of solace in the heart of nature's creations was so therapeutic! I spent all morning revelling in their beauty, variety and total peace ... a very rare treat!

Singapore

From Cairns, we flew to Brisbane and caught a plane to our only stop-over on the way back home - Singapore. We were taken by taxi to our hotel and the next day we strolled through the streets and bridges of this independent city-state on the south tip of the Malay Peninsula, separating the Indian Ocean from the South China Sea. It appears spotless, very well organized and rich in history. Its symbol is the Merlion - a mythical creature with a lion's head and the body of a fish spouting water into the Marina Bay overlooking the spectacular Marina Bay Sands Hotel and the lotus-shaped Art Science Museum.

Next to it, the towering Supertrees construction offering a light and music show at night. Our walk was suddenly interrupted by an almighty thunder - everyone ran for shelter under one of the concrete bridges ... but nothing happened. We continued our sightseeing to Chinatown Centre, Little India and finished in THE Raffles - the two fan palms signalling its entrance. We went straight upstairs to the iconic Long Bar to sample the Singapore Sling - the traditional cocktail of gin, heering cherry brandy, grenadine, pineapple, and lime juice – the same routine as 35 years ago - memories ... The only change was the refurbished hotel and the refreshed gardens - the atmosphere remained the same: the colonial decor and the turban clad doorman welcoming the guests and the interested tourists.

At night we went on a Night Safari in the local zoological gardens. First in a Jeep, then by foot, we played explorers hunting the beasts with our cameras. The result was quite stunning and we managed to catch some nocturnal creatures.

The next day was the last day of our adventure: the Changi airport - one of the busiest in the world had a lot to offer, from the tropical gardens and the butterfly farm to a swimming pool, the highest slide and masses of massaging armchairs - the perfect relaxation for the tired, stressed and simply bored while waiting for the flight home.

All that is in addition to endless shopping malls, international cuisine spots and miles of walking space. And spotless as everywhere on the island, famous for a total prohibition of using chewing gum! Quite an experience!

CHAPTER II

AS TIME GOES BY...

The reality kicks in, and the dream becomes a reality. The time comes to reflect on past events, giving one a springboard to take-off and grab life by its horns ... Living in Poland in a restrictive system based on socialist principles needed a lot of resilience and determination to reach the surface and achieve anything. The system was corrupt and based on who, not what you know. A party membership opened most doors to many walks of life and many joined for precisely that reason. Everywhere one went, preference was given to the party members and their families. From food coupons in the critical years to flat and car allocations were based on this requirement. Similarly, the youth organised in party units was privileged in choosing the schools and gaining points for their working-class background. The universities accepted applications for courses from everybody but the ones in greatest demand often allowed the students from farming and factory workers' families to take places regardless of capabilities, as the general trend was to include the proletariat in every field of life at the expense of the intelligentsia.

The results were often disappointing and detrimental to the stability of the equality principle. The cultural tradition focused on a family unit with matriarchal leadership, but equal rights for all members; there were no prejudices regarding men and women working on an equal basis, contributing equally both personally and workwise to the family unit. There was a very well-developed network of state-run nurseries, kindergartens and schools with equal opportunities for all. And education was obligatory till the age of 18, with 14 subjects on the curriculum to be completed by all - regardless of individual preferences to the level of GCSEs. Those included two foreign languages (for obvious political reasons, Russian and a western language) and military training as the Cold War was in full swing and we were primed to defend ourselves in case of a nuclear war - started, of course by the rotten capitalist enemy - to the point of learning to construct a nuclear shelter. The other side of political paranoia.

To be able to get some information regarding the world, we were glued for hours to the radio station Free Europe based in Luxemburg, desperate for some news but that diverse source was also controlled and often the sound was masked with the buzzing noises. Some travelled abroad to the West and brought the papers, records and stories about so-called normal life. There were many exchanges with the schools and colleges on the eastern side in the obvious attempt to unify the Eastern Bloc youngsters with varying effects. Some of us came back horrified by the level of poverty in some places, but happy that the costs of the journey could be paid back by selling our clothes to our hosts at sky-high costs.

And when we tried to oppose the authorities, we were locked up at school and had to wait for our parents to collect us. Those who courageously dared to take their grievances to the streets paid dearly with incarceration and loss of rights.

The dream of going west prevailed for many, and once all was ready, my adventure was on ... My experiences in England, Spain and New

Zealand taught me many things I would not have had a chance to learn at home. Primarily, patience, tolerance and heightened social awareness. The fact that I could speak the languages in the respective countries was a gate-opener to many possibilities and understanding of the workings of each country. A great tool for establishing lasting contact with others, and for maintaining a healthy body and healthy mind.

The first observation I made in England was the class system and the fact that it has been very strict and well-established for centuries. The south- north divide is especially striking. The prominent ruling classes centred in London and the Home Counties, and the working-class force was scattered all over northern England. And it is obvious that the privileged are primed from a very early age to be the elite of the nation and lead it to its lost glory. The schooling system is the best reflection of this: the private boarding schools are very selective in admitting the pupils: the costlier, the higher in society.

Then comes the Eton elite, and finally, the Golden Triangle of Oxford, Cambridge and London universities - the academic moulders of the lucky ones who survived their stringent selection. The rest are educated in public and comprehensive-government- run - schools, and it is only recently that the onus for admissions to the top educational establishments has changed to a more inclusive mode.

This patriarchal society bathed in Victorian traditions is staggeringly unequal. Although combining all races, religions and beliefs - this island has been a shelter to many alternatively thinking individuals - there is a sublime underlying feeling of English superiority. It must be the result of 200 years of ruling the waves and conquering the world and its riches - Britannia is still at the top ... It is obvious to any foreigner who is looked down upon the moment he/she opens their mouth and the accent gives them away. The fact that you come from a different country with a different language and culture - where you spent years learning English as it has established itself over centuries as an international trade language - is totally irrelevant. In fact, despite having an accent, I was told my English is better than the natives as I know grammar and speak grammatically!

On the other hand, I heard comments re my speech therapy sessions when, much to my surprise, I was questioned how I could "teach to speak someone proper with my accent" - no comment on ignorance. But I must admit the communication skills between professionals - intentionally or unintentionally - leave a lot to be desired.

Total amazement appears on English faces when you disclose that you speak - and communicate in - four languages, which are equally, if not more, used all over the world.

But there are exceptions in this insular community. And thanks to one open-minded lady, I was given a chance to study at the London university department - a rarity in those years, as I was accepted after one interview and offered a place on an exclusively English course which opened the professional gates to me all over the world. My personal success reached its culminating peak during the graduation ceremony at the Royal Albert Hall in London, where thousands celebrated our academic trophies. I was the only Pole with a Master in Science - and so proud that despite all the adversities, I managed to surface unscathed and triumphant. A diploma from any English university speaks louder than any other out there!

I have experienced unbelievable gender inequality. Starting with women's lower earnings and social rights (interestingly, England was the first country to introduce voting rights for women) as the old-fashioned mentality prevails.

When I became a self-employed professional, I did my tax returns religiously following the instructions as per the tax office leaflet. After a while, I found out that my husband could buy a Porsche car and include it in his expenses but I was not even allowed to include my childminding expenses which were incurred exclusively during my working hours! And I had to work to support my family to avoid scrounging off the state ... It is a man's world and the penpushers regulate our lives with their gain in mind. And not only the civil service lot without real social strife awareness; the majority of them were born with a silver spoon in their mouth and followed their upbringing values and their predecessors' paths.

It was also clear that apart from many walks of life ridden with inequality, there was a serious discrimination issue and a hush-hush policy within the health service. It became apparent to me when my Down Syndrome daughter was born at the leading University of Cambridge hospital. The fact about her condition was conveyed by a consultant paediatrician, who announced in a parochial voice that I "don't have to take her home - she will not do anything anyway" was a total shock ... as if the general trend was to get rid of those peaceful, emotionally supreme and fantastic life companions. Yet the social burden of alcoholics, drug addicts and simple time wasters was of more importance ... Sad but true, which I experienced when my alcoholic ex-husband destroyed the family by losing two houses and left me literally in the street with three children.

Later, when the time came to find a suitable place for my fantastic daughter, I encountered more discrimination, both personally and against her. The local authorities - in their supreme know-how and total lack of knowledge about such children - refused me a place in a local village school. It took three meetings and my socialist red-tape jumping skills and determination to change their minds. The result was stunning, and it opened doors and others' minds to many other children who happened to be differently able and yet as successful as mine is.

Another anomaly, in my opinion, was the lack of cooperation between the school and the parents. I have always believed that raising children should be a unified front of parents and educationalists. As a teacher myself, I approached the schools regarding concerning issues which were aired at home first and then relayed to the respective teacher. The result was very strange and disappointing. Any matter requiring a teacher's support was gently swept under the carpet, and I was informed that the matter was being dealt with. The bullying continued. The effect was very sad as the children were told to inform the school of any problems at home, but parental intervention was overlooked and, in our case, led to disastrous ends. One was used as a scapegoat in a drug-selling affair in her private school (bursary supported) which ended in her not the culprit's tears and removal just before her GCSEs; another had to deal on her own with a very disruptive Down Syndrome pupil who bullied her so much that she developed a true phobia (the four-page letter to the headmistress had no effect).

And finally, the third was classified as nearly an adult, and I was informed that she was receiving support at school which led to her announcement that she could report me to social services! With that I gave up the so-called educational places and decided that it is time to set up a Royal Association for Abused Parents - this shocked my nearly-an-adult daughter and stopped her in her tracks - the mother had rights as well! And this contrasted with my upbringing with a total focus on the family, respect for each, and supportive to, with special reverence towards the older generation.

Life in England has become a battleground for me standing up for my and my daughter's rights. The number of indifferent, uninvolved and detached professionals I came across was worrying. Lots of them were pseudo- professionals focusing on their own gains and not the people they were paid to help. Lack of care, empathy and insight were staggering.

But - as they say - you win some and you lose some. On the whole, it has been a very educational and horizon-widening lesson. It also showed me that the maxim "who you know" does not always apply - there are many cases where common sense and human tolerance can lead to great successes - as where there is a will, there is a way ... always!

CHAPTER 12

HISPANIC ADVENTURE AND ANTARCTICA IN THE SOUTHERN HEMISPHERE

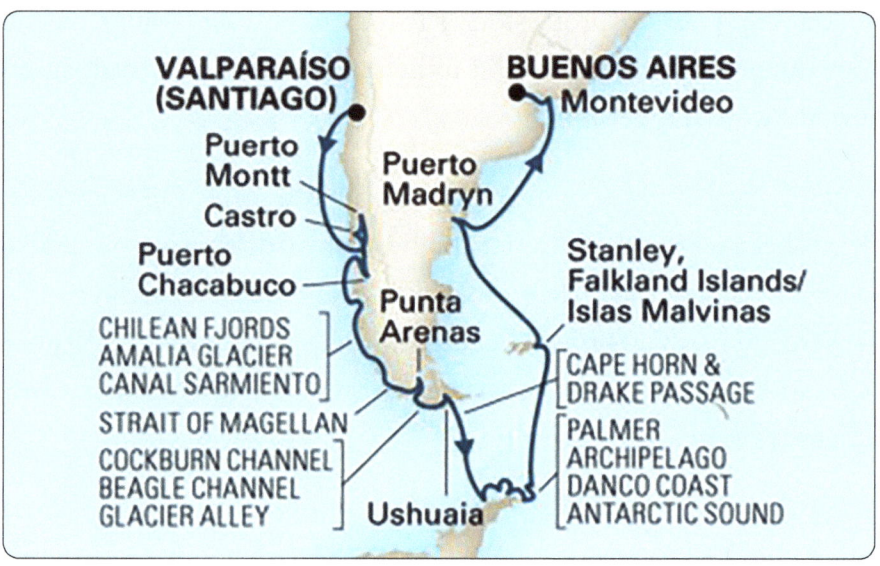

My fascination with everything Spanish started with my godmother, who - in socialist Poland - was one of the few fluent speakers of the language. She acted as an interpreter on business trips organised by various chemical departments wanting to trade and travelled all over the Hispanic territories, bringing back captivating stories and developing my taste for similar experiences.

My direct contact started with a group of doctors from Zaragoza on a trip to the most important places in Poland. I loved their vibrant personalities, sense of humour and zest for life.

At university, I was given a choice of selecting an additional language and I chose Spanish. And that was it: geography, history - both the positive and the negative, internal and international politics of the Hispanic world. My dream was to experience the theory and the time came when we could make it true ...

The expectations were high. The excitement was even higher.

Chile

THE COLONIAL CAPITAL AND ITS HIDDEN JEWEL

We flew from Heathrow to Benitez Airport Santiago. To acclimatise, we spent three days in a lovely hotel to get the feel of the place. The capital sits in a valley surrounded by the snow-capped Andes and the Chilean Coast Range. There are lots of architectural remnants from colonial times and the nearby Valparaiso offers an artistic feast. This "Little San Francisco" is full of colourful cliff-top houses, reachable by lifts and steep funiculars, and is proud of La Sebastiana - the quirky former residence-turned-museum of the Nobel Prize winner poet Pablo Neruda.

The Jewel of the Pacific, as it is also known, is full of contrasts: Bohemian, dilapidated, colourful and poetic, hard-working port with ritzy and hippie beaches. Not far are world-famous vineyards where we bought a bottle of Santa Ema wine - still unopened, waiting for Emma's 40th birthday.

CRUISING OFF ALONG THE CHILEAN ANDIES

The voyage started from there in the late afternoon as we waved Adios! to the spectacularly beautiful city and sailed away on our round-the-South- America-and-Antarctica cruise. After a day at sea, we had the usual inspection of the ship to orientate ourselves with the layout and the programmes on offer. And the choice was plentiful. For those with a scientific interest, there were lectures conducted by mature explorers familiar with the wilderness and the challenges of living in arid conditions. The shows, restaurants and evening games suited everybody's tastes ... Just relax and enjoy it ...

PORT MONTT

Our first stop was in Puerto Montt (or MeliPulli in the local Mapuche tribe dialect which means "Four Hills"), a lovely, relaxed place which gave us the first taste of rural Chilean life. Founded in 1853 by German settlers, it became the gateway to the Chilean Lake District and the fjords of Patagonia. It is a picturesque port overlooked by the Osorno volcano with a very interesting food market - the variety of local herbs on offer is limitless and the locals revel in these heaps of mother nature's gifts. We were staying away from these specialities ... you never know ... It is famous for salmon aquaculture and its Mapuche craftworks, modern seafront, attractive restaurants and breathtaking views of the Pacific.

CASTRO – CHILE'S THIRD OLDEST CITY

Castro was next - located on Chiloe Island, and famous for its palafitos - a rainbow assortment of colourful houses built on stilts. Once the home of thousands of farmers and a target for European pirates, the commune is very cosmopolitan and recently surged as a culinary place attracting the best of the world's refined palates. It is also close to the Chiloe National Park and the Darwin's Route trail where you can enjoy the humid forest, which amazed Darwin in his exploration of the island. But he classified it a possible charming place but for the detestable climate..

CHACABUCO

Next day Chacabuco in the Atacama Desert was the third stop - nowadays a ghost town, but a very important nitrate producer at the beginning of the 20th century and built with English, American and Chilean labour. It was later used by Pinochet as a concentration camp for his opposition leaders and he surrounded the place with landmines to avoid any escapes - they are still being found in the area.

SAILING SOUTH

Following our visit to the port, we were in for three days of mother nature's wonders sailing along the Pacific coast. We had an opportunity to admire Chilean fjords, glaciers through the Sarmiento - a principal Patagonia channel sailed by the local Kawesqar people for more than 6000 years.

Then the Strait of Magellan - the most important natural sea passage between the Pacific and Atlantic oceans, separating South America from Tierra del Fuego. It was discovered in 1520 by a Portuguese explorer who was the first to circumnavigate the Earth. The largest city Punta Arenas - the city of the red roofs - is full of reminders of the region's discovery and known for its European and Russian immigrants. It was also a penal colony where all the relapsing offenders were involved in the construction of the famous railway running all the way to Santiago. Rich in oil, gold and sheep farming, it is of great geopolitical importance because of its proximity to Antarctica.

Argentina

The next day we woke up in the world's southernmost city of Ushuaia on the island of the Land of Fire - the Argentinian property. The end of the world pier is the major port of departure for commercial and tourist expeditions to the Antarctic Peninsula and the Falkland Islands.

Place is very picturesque, surrounded by the Andes and its glaciers and famous for the naval ship ARA General Belgrano, which sailed from there during the Falklands war and was sunk by the British fleet. The monument was erected in its memory in 1992.

BRAVING DRAKE PASSAGE

And so we sailed away in the evening towards Antarctica. The captain informed us about the challenges of sailing the Drake Passage past Cape Horn. It is considered the most treacherous stretch of water as the currents have no land resistance and the waves can reach 40 feet. It is also known as the most powerful convergence of the seas. As we travelled a lot on the seas, we took his warning lightly.

Well, we all err, and this time it was our turn: two days of stomach-churning see-saw experience. With the china plates and the cutlery being substituted by plastic ones, the balancing acts to keep the food on the plate were easier to manage. Everybody seemed to be affected by either seasickness or balancing problems. Our brains were in total confusion as to the place and time ... We were sailing on a cruiser with 5000 souls on its decks, but it felt like a walnut shell being thrust up and down and side to side by a mountain stream! And when it stopped, we all sighed with relief ... the captain was the first to do so ... And to think that explorers like Shackleton and Wild braved these waters in tiny vessels - courage unsung.

Antarctica

THE CONTINENT OF SUPERLATIVES

After the storm comes the calm ... This biblical statement proved true after a totally disorientating experience. The recovery took a while, but all is well that ends well. From now on, we hoped for plain sailing...

We sped towards the Antarctic Peninsula pass the Palmer Archipelago discovered by a Belgian explorer and his mate Roald Amundsen on board the Belgica, through the treacherous Antarctic Sound - a deceptive and difficult to traverse stretch of water – first navigated by Swedish Captain Larsen in 1902.

The place was full of floating ice formations slowly growing in size and becoming fascinating in forms – a paradise for a photographer. Needless to say, I sat by our cabin porthole with my camera and started shooting.

The sky was grey. Initially, we passed by various ice floes, gradually increasing in size shaped by the wind and the water. On approaching the continent they increased in all shapes and sizes with occasional seal hitch- hikers taking a free ride on the bergs and starring at us in bewilderment – the crowds of adventure seekers shaking due to cold winds on the decks, hoping for that special picture of this apparently calm and nature-ruled vast spread of white ... Through Palmer Arch along the Danco Coast, admiring the beauty, stillness and wilderness...

Three days of white rocky landscape with occasional visits to endless fjords – weather permitting.

We had to navigate through various straits and look out for any signs of Antarctic fauna. We observed a rookery of penguins - Macaroni or Rockhoppers - on the bare shores; we looked up at the mountains and their glaciers splitting with a characteristic blue crack due to compressed ice. Passengers and crew were in awe: it is a memorable experience watching the stunning glacier designs decorating the surrounding peaks – the absolute silence of more than 3000 spectators is deafening! And all that in full sunshine reflecting on the slopes with glittering effect – as in an enchanted fairyland ...

The visit was enriched by the lectures of an ex-explorer from the McMurdo polar station – the largest one in Antarctica, set up on a bare volcanic rock in 1955 by the USA. The stories were captivating and the place was worth a direct approach but, unfortunately, the scientists do not welcome nosy tourists.

The nearby active volcano Mt. Erebus provides another scientific opportunity: it was examined by a robotic explorer Dante I in 1992, which marked the first robotic expedition in Antarctica. It aimed to investigate the persistent lava lake inside the craters and acquire samples of magma, but the optic cable fault defeated the plan.

Our route along the continent took us to the Antarctic Sound – abundant in bird colonies, Adelie and Emperor penguin waddles - their unique habitat. The tabular icebergs added to the dramatic environment allowing us to snap every icily attractive creation as we passed by them ... Some were bigger than our cruiser, floating majestically on the ocean, displaying nature's absolute power over us. They looked different from every angle, changing colour with changing daylight and impressing us with the variety ...

And so we continued till the night fell. The next day was at sea; time to relax, check the photos and film, edit them and get ready for the next stop: the Falkand Islands.

The Falkland Islands

... OR ISLAS MALVINAS

The tumultuous history of this archipelago involves the British, Spanish, French and again British ownership for nearly 200 years. Judging by the historical treaties it should have been allowed to fly the Argentinian flag, but the matter is still a bone of contention between the countries.

We were approaching the capital Port Stanley and found out that cruise ships were not allowed to dock there; we were tendered to the port in 20 minutes. It was a dreary, wet day with the clouds hanging low and the locals welcoming us wholeheartedly and inviting to the tourist shop to warm up and spend our pennies.

We did so gladly, and then went for a short walk to the 1982 Liberation Memorial founded entirely by the islanders to commemorate the

British victory and the forces that helped to free the island from the Argentine occupation.

The visit to the Gentoo penguin colony was second on the agenda. We were transported by Jeeps across the island with a running commentary on the events of that unfortunate conflict and shown the strategic places where blood was shed in the name of pride. The penguins – the fastest of the species with the capability of lasting seven minutes underwater - were peacefully oblivious to our presence, strutting their stuff and minding their business. Some younger creatures in tuxedoes were so inquisitive they came closer and posed for the photos with grace and model know-how. The noise volume was overbearing and we departed soon, wondering where the snow was as the beach was as barren as the rest of the island.

ARGENTINIAN EXPERIENCE

After a day at sea sailing north-west we reached the eastern coast of the South American continent. We were back in Argentina in Puerto Madryn, located on the northern coast of Patagonia, and the star destination for marine wildlife watching. Founded in 1865 by Welsh immigrants, it attracts tourists with its Magellan penguin colonies, whales, orcas, and seals. It is also a UNESCO World Heritage Site as it is a doorway to Atlantic Patagonia. A short visit to the town because we had to get back to the ship earlier, as they were trying to make up the time lost in Antarctica.

The ride was a smooth one – we continued enjoying the entertainment on board, the food in the self-service buffet, the delicacies offered in the elegant restaurants, and the deck activities as the temperature was rising steadily. With two days at sea, we watched an ice sculpting show, shapes carved from a variety of fruits which were amazing in figures and complexity, quizzes and evening discos on the main deck – a must for dancing-loving Emma!

Back in Argentina

BUENOS AIRES WELCOME

We docked in Fair Winds capital at midday. It was hot – the climatic change from the south was shocking. As it was the end of the cruise, we disembarked and were transported to the hotel we had booked to stay for a couple of extra days. Thank God for air-conditioning - first hours were spent in front of the old-fashioned blower trying to cool down.

I decided to go shopping in the nearby market. I was getting the feel of this city of faded European grandeur and Latin passion. The streets shaded by indigenous trees, magnificent monuments and endless cafes ... It is cosmopolitan, vibrant, and famous for its proud traditions of tango, football, and mate - a pungent South American caffeine rich infused beverage from the yerba mate tree similar to the English holly. The metropolis had to be seen to appreciate its strong identity - it never sleeps and mesmerizes visitors.

The tour started at the Plaza de Mayo – the founding centre of BA in 1885 with its Casa Rosada: a stately balconied mansion which is the residence of the Argentinian president and one of the most emblematic buildings in the capital. Then we drove to see the Evita monument, passing by the endless art galleries, science museums and observatories. Eva Peron – the wife of President Juan Peron

- was honoured for her relentless fight for improving the women's rights and living conditions of the poor labourers, herself coming from poverty. She was given the title of "A Spiritual Leader of the Nation" by the parliament.

From there we went to Caminito in the artistic neighbourhood of La Boca. This complete change of mood was very welcome: the colourful street museum looked enchanting in the sunset, reflecting the city seductive and bustling with electric energy and character. It is here where the tango was born. Luckily, we could watch it in El Viejo Almacen in many versions during the night show with a glass of prime champagne... What a sexy and engaging performance ... There is no end to dance variables ... the choreography was spectacular!

Next stop was at the pride and glory of this football-obsessed nation: Armando stadium named by the 16 million fans La Bombonera ("The Box of Chocolates"). With memorabilia of its most precious child No 10 Diego Maradona – all in the club colours of blue and yellow. From there we were whisked to Puerto Madero and shown the Women's Bridge; a rotating footbridge of a striking asymmetrical design, which is supposed to represent a couple dancing tango. It is a visual highlight in this renovated commercial and residential centre, spanning the harbour since 2001 and looking like a needle with harp-like cables since. Finally, we arrived at the Plaza de la República to see the national historic monument and the icon of Buenos Aires, the Obelisk, which was erected in 1936 to commemorate the 400th anniversary of the first Spanish settlement on the Rio de la Plata. Currently the centre point for all celebrations of the portenos – the people of this port.

The next day I ventured to see the spread-about architectural treasures by foot – Emma stayed in the hotel room enjoying the cool. The humidity was oppressive, but it did not stop me from snapping more architectural jewels to add to my collection and appreciating this massive metropolis known for welcoming migrants from every corner of the world ... the international mix is overwhelming. So using every minute of the last hours, I was wandering the streets and trying to absorb it all.

Until we reached the airport, we coded EZE in the IATA language. Then another chapter opened: Emma started coughing and did so all the way to London. All 14 hours of it. I was worried for her and for my fellow passengers as the majority wanted to catch a couple of winks during this long and arduous journey. But she could not stop. We were offered a supply of oxygen – she refused. On arrival at Heathrow I was seriously concerned and took her straight away to the surgery. Her oxygen levels were two-thirds low, she was exhausted from flying and coughing and the only option was a transfer to the hospital. The ambulance was called and we zoomed to the A&E department. The diagnosis was bilateral pneumonia which needed an infusion of two antibiotics.

The major concern was whether she could battle the infection with her suppressed immune system, which is a common characteristic of the Down Syndrome population. She did, and much to everybody's relief, she was back home within two weeks, looking her usual self, although somewhat weaker ...

CHAPTER 13

MY MISSION...

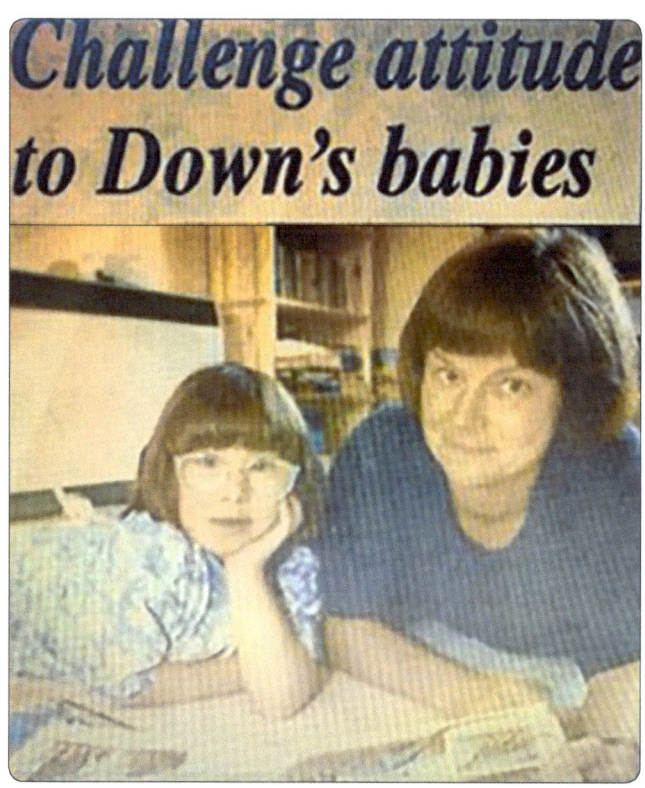

My first article in the local newspaper...

We were back to life, back to reality ... this time with a big bump!

Life was slowly returning to its old normal – if that concept exists at all. Caroline was settled in Cambridge teaching

English in a private language school. Sophie was facing the challenges of being a nurse and we were following the broken routine of Emma's art sessions in Cambridge. Both the College and the Rowan studio welcomed her very enthusiastically ... she loved it to the full!

My Mission Explained ...

In the meantime, I came across some articles in the national press regarding issues that people with Down syndrome encountered in society, including social ostracism, educational integration difficulties, health problems and psychological insecurities. I remembered my attempt to change people's attitude locally, when Emma attended our local village primary school through an article published in the press. The aim was to address my predicament, stemming from the observation of the school environment in relation to Emma and her treatment by staff and peers. I strongly believe that despite social prejudice and marginalisation of the different, everybody deserves a chance to access the possibilities of the social facilities on offer. And everybody deserves a chance to try to succeed. If not, the alternative options are in place – but give people like Emma a chance!

Since her birth in the Cambridge University leading teaching hospital, where I was told I "do not have to take her home as she will not do anything," her life path has been laid with cobblestones, starting with her unfortunate and negligent discharge from the hospital with a malformed heart, and needing serious open heart surgery two years later. Having recovered from the trauma, she was a smiling and loving individual with visible potential, who deserved an ordinary chance in life. But the social reality was not welcoming. The bureaucratic policies and blinkered officials were very reluctant to give her an opportunity to join the club: I was twice refused enrolment at the local nursery as "it was not the council's policy" to integrate such children. My determination won her a place and she fitted in with a support worker with no problems. Similarly, the primary and secondary education managers were not helpful, but with gentle persuasion and reference to her human rights, they took the risk. The result was more than satisfactory: Emma left her college with a GCSE in Art!

... and Going International

My mission has mostly been successful with the production of my educational documentary entitled "the sky is the limit". I have decided that the most effective medium of communication nowadays is via visual input. The life story of Emma includes ups and downs with minimal commentary at the beginning of the 25-minute film and at its end says it all. The rest was compiled from family pictures and videos to show Emma's experiences, character and zest for life. My friend's husband put it together - including the background sound - and a year later we had a finished product ready to spread the word in the world.

Since its completion, the documentary has been submitted to more than 300 international film festivals, and awarded 50 prizes and distinctions from Hawaii to Bhutan. The first award came from Chile: I was the winner of the best first film director category and felt so honoured to be awarded my first laurel in South America.

The USA was very generous in its recognition: from the Hollywood Film Competition giving us a diamond award for the best doc to other Californian, Delaware, New Mexico, Kentucky, Pennsylvania, Illinois, New York and Hawaii festivals. In West Virginia, we won CARE Awards.

Great Britain reacted at the Pinewood Film Festival and London Circle of Directors. Scotland rewarded us at Glasgow Film Festival. Later came more European prizes and selections. Then there were European selections and awards from Spain, France, Belgium, Italy, Poland, Russia and Turkey. Even Asia responded with recognition in Philippines, Indonesia (Human Rights), Bhutan, India, and we reached as far as New Zealand.

We have covered the world! And that was my idea ... to introduce a positive and socially challenging theme – the reaction was astounding, and it is still continuing ...

We are off to Mexico!

Our direct experience of a film festival came when Oaxaca Film Festival in Mexico selected our film for screening, which was to be followed by a question time session. The festival organized our accommodation and transport to the venues, so all we had to do was enjoy Mexican hospitality and exotic food, and soak up the diverse atmosphere of the place and the festival. This unique experience made a very special mark on our life. For the first time, we were going to watch our film on a large screen in the company of cinephiles from all over the world and face them directly during the Qs time.

But first, a little of the local folklore: we were taken to do a bit of sightseeing to the Old Town, starting with a visit to the Cathedral

- a baroque ecclesiastical church - one of the most beautiful ones in Mexico and famous for its complex layout, monastery and impressive native iconography overlaying the Catholic symbols following an extensive restoration in the 90s. We were shown the cloisters and told stories of the old affluent families paying small fortunes for their mature daughters to be kept there – a privilege only allowable to the few. Each of them was commemorated in a large display of portraits adorning the walls. The place was very spiritual and a local Mexican orchestra made the visit ...

Next, we stopped at the market passing by various restaurants, cafes and incredible examples of local flora; one caught my eye, as I have never seen such complexity of Mother Nature's design anywhere: the Red Rooster crest plant - totally jaw-droping!!

Then a glass of the local drink called *tejate* – exclusive to the region and popular among Aztec rulers and Zapotec gods from pre-Hispanic times. It is a non-alcoholic mixture of ground toasted maize, fermented cocoa beans and local flowers – the drink of Gods...

Delicious! After roaming the streets and the local craftwork shops, we reached Constitution Square and were treated to the music coming from the bandstand – opposite the Gothic town hall where our documentary was to be screened the next day. We were waiting with much anticipation, and when the time came we sat in the front row holding hands and squeezing each other with excitement. The film was one of the sets of four and received great applause.

I was asked to join the other directors to face the audience and answered many questions – followed by numerous handshakes with the spectators on the way out. We were shining on the international stage - indescribable!

The next day was free, so we popped round to the local market to enjoy fresh smoothies made on the premises, and a variety of breads – all handmade from local ingredients. The evening was reserved for the Gala - our festival experience was coming to an end. We gathered in a large conference room in downtown Oaxaca and met masses of participating directors, producers and all involved in making independent filmmaking count ... What a night ...!

And the homecoming was like waking up from a dream ... home sweet home awaiting...

CHAPTER 14

ROUTE 66 FOR MY 66TH

All 4000 km of it!

The years flew by and my 66th birthday was approaching, much to my surprise, at cosmic speed... One of my dreams on my bucket list was to follow Route 66 which encompassed many places I had been to before in the USA. It would also help me with keeping my word given to Emma that one day I would take her to the old places I visited with little Caroline. This was my great chance.

My idea was to travel a distance of nearly 4000 km on a three-wheeler, a Harley Davidson with a guide, but it was quickly changed after calculating the time it would have taken us to cover the Main Street of America. The very appropriate present was to materialize using a coach trip company which took us and 50 other Brits from Chicago in Illinois all the way to Santa Monica beach in California in two weeks.

The route is the quintessential embodiment of the road and its greatest promises for the Americans; freedom and serendipity, kitsch and living history and a study of their history and drive eastward. It runs across the eight mid states of America - Illinois, Missouri, Kansas, Oklahoma, Texas, New Mexico, Arizona and California; it was the main highway for the travellers West from 1926 till 1985. And the diagonal trip takes in the country's most archetypal roadside scenes. Neon lights, rusty in the middle - of - nowhere truck stops or kitschy Americana – it has it all ...

Illinois

CHICAGO

Our adventure started in the Windy City of Al Capone fame ... at the very point of the historic Route 66 at the base of the Willis Tower (previously the Sears Tower) rising above C h i c a g o with all its 110 floors – the highest building in the city. Before leaving the place, we were treated to a short sightseeing tour which included a visit to the famous public sculpture Cloud Gate, nicknamed the Bean, with its reflecting surface inspired by liquid mercury. The inside surface warps and multiplies reflections - a practising ground for any photographer. Later we joined the firemen and their museum commemorating the Chicago fire in 1871, which burned most of the town. In the afternoon we went on the Chicago River trip to admire a fantastic collection of architectural competition pieces: every building with its individual features - some even defying gravity laws. A true feast for glass- building fans. And its 37 movable bridges spread across the river are equally attractive.

Later, we watched the elongating skyscrapers' shadows spreading over Lake Michigan from the 64th floor, and in the late afternoon sun embarked on a boat, which took us out on the lake to watch the sunset – unforgettable...

The next day the wake-up call came far too early; after a quick breakfast, we boarded the coach and hit the road to get our kicks from Route 66. We drove through town enjoying the Halloween displays in front of historic houses, the sun was rising and revealing the Navy Pier, the Field Museum - home of the largest and best preserved Tyrannosaurus Rex called Sue after her discoverer - and Adler Planetarium with the monument of the Polish astronomer who "steadied the sun and made the earth go round it", Nicolaus Copernicus – a replica of the monument standing outside the Science Academy in Warsaw.

The road ran through flat plains, at times only parallel to its original track, as parts of the Mother Road were neglected in the past and needed an alternative to continue the traditional path.

ODELL

The first rest was at the Standard Oil Gas Station, putting us in the Route 66 mood. Built in 1932 in Odell, Illinois, the house with a canopy served the customers during the heyday of travel on Route 66. The sign still swings from the roof in the warm breeze and the old-fashioned pump is restored and ready to serve the customers again ...

PONTIAC

The Route 66 Museum in Pontiac continued the story ... and the local Pontiac Automobile Museum spiced it up with the original vintage cars (the biggest collection of Pontiac and Oakland makes in the country) and Route 66 memorabilia, including the biggest mural of its shield outside.

SPRINGFIELD

The state capital welcomed us in full sunshine. The Capitol State Building offered a much-desired shelter and we had a chance to focus on the heart of American political history.

And the elaborate decor of the place was built in 1868 in a French Renaissance-style; its dome is covered with colourful stainedglass patterns, and inside the House, the Senate and the Court Chambers are generously decorated with paintings and sculptures.

The home of the 16th American president Abraham Lincoln before he left for the White House is full of his memorabilia. The house he lived in with his family is well preserved, and a historical place where the future president Abe Lincoln spent his early adult years, his tomb frequented by many for good luck. His bronze head has a distinctive light patch on his nose – the memento of rubbings by the visitors.

NEW SALEM

The next day we were driven to New Salem – the reconstructed historical site where Lincoln lived as a young adult. We got off the coach and went to the cafe; on the door, there was a sign stating guns were prohibited ... We had never seen anything like it but quickly realized that, after all, we were on the way to the wild west.

The state park was opened in 1921 and all the memorabilia and replicas were gathered to commemorate Lincoln's stay in the village, where he worked as a boatman, a postmaster, a railway splitter and made his first political steps to the Illinois General Assembly.

The sun was intense, so we welcomed the shady place full of log houses, cabins, shops and businesses furnished with implements, furniture and period costumed interpreters giving full accounts of life in the village.

The next attraction was linked closely to our themed tour. We were shown the Chain of Rocks Bridge: the giant rusty construction spans the Mississippi River with a 22-degree bend in the middle - the old Route 66 bridge nowadays only allows pedestrians and cyclists.

Time was short, so we headed back to Springfield and prepared for the next stretch of the Mother Road.

Missouri

On the way, we had some interesting stopovers in the Show-Me State. The first one - and the most refreshing one - was at the Drewes Frozen Custard parlour founded in 1929. We could refresh our palates with a custard ice cream. The spirits were lifted and we moved on to the Transport Museum - a collection of 450 electric, steam and diesel-powered trains showing the importance of transport in the development of the States. Absolute treasury, with full access to most of the exhibits, and a chance to get a ride in some of them ... my kind of place...

From there, we moved on to the classic Route 66 diner, where they served the classic American hamburgers and fries with thick shakes in a fully traditional restaurant from the 50s - it was like watching the movie Grease... The decor, the service and the atmosphere ...

The cherry on the cake that day was added in the late afternoon, when we arrived at the Fantastic Caverns. The drive-through caverns were discovered by the local athletic women's club – 12 ladies in all – in 1867. The blend of stone, water and time has created this geological marvel, which can be studied by travelling for more than an hour at the back of the Jeep.

The beauty of the formations is stunning; some endangered local fauna species such as a cavefish fish, a crayfish and a grotto salamander live there as well in the lower part, inaccessible to visitors. They are all tiny, colourless, and blind, having lived in the darkness for generations.

ST. LOUIS

We slept at the Drury Hotel, and in the morning started exploring the city. It sits on the western bank of the Mississippi River, which divides the two states of Illinois and Missouri.

Founded by French fur traders, it flourished and now is a thriving multicultural port, also famous as a centre for medicine and biotechnology. We walked all over the place poking our noses into the opened impressive structures such as the Basilica, the Library, the Courthouse, and finally, the Gateway Arch. This symbol towering over the city was something else. Once we discovered it was possible to go to the top and revel in the views over the river and further afield, we joined the queue.

Very soon, we were squashed in a four-seater tram capsule zooming upwards and feeling claustrophobic... all forgotten very soon as the panorama was breath-taking and on a sunny day the visibility was perfect – the resulting photos as well. The Arch celebrates the American expansion to the west and is dedicated to the American people. It became a symbol of St. Louis and the most visited attraction in the world - rightly so!

When we had enough of the arched floor and the height of 200m above sea level, we went down to get some lunch. Just as well, stocking up with fat and calories before visiting the piece de resistance, the Budweiser Brewery.

This 19th-century oldest and largest complex, built in a Romanesque style in 1875, allows a first-hand look at the heritage and timeless tradition; the Clydesdale horses, tastings and a classic beer garden where its 25 brands can be tasted in these historic surroundings. The Budweiser horses, which used to pull the wagons with beer barrels, can be observed in their training field. The Brew House is ornate with multi-storey hop chandeliers, intricate ironwork and the use of natural light - a combination of glass, metal and human imagination – a piece of unique industrial art.

Oklahoma

From the geographical centre of the USA in the Missouri Plains we drove through Oklahoma Great Plains, the state known for severe weather. The name derives from the Chocktaw tribal words "okla" and "humma" meaning "red people." In fact, 25 Native American languages are spoken in the state. Its economy encompasses the production of natural gas, oil and agriculture. It also relies on aviation, energy and biotechnology.

OKLAHOMA CITY

The capital lies in the middle of an active oil field and oil derricks dot the capital's ground. It was made famous by Nat King Cole in the song "Get Your Kicks On Route 66". Another interesting fact is that it has been struck by 13 tornadoes to date. And in 1995, a bomb was detonated in front of the main government building: the 10-floor construction collapsed, killing 168 people. The culprit was executed by lethal injection.

The ruins were removed, and the site was made the Oklahoma City National Memorial. The reflecting pool is flanked by two large gates with the times of explosion start and end. On its side, there are 168 symbolic bronze and stone chairs; they represent empty chairs at the family tables - the children's ones are smaller.

On the other side of the pool there is a survivor tree, which was part of the landscape around the building and survived the blast and the fire which followed. The whole complex is very quiet and ethereal. It is decorated with children's drawings, tiles and sculptures to commemorate the anniversary of the blast every year on April 19.

After the solemn visit, we returned to the hotel and planned an early night as departure times were scheduled for the very early morning. However, our wishful thinking was blown away by a hurricane with a monsoon-like rainfall. The music reaching us was intense and loud - the rain kept us awake and glued to the windows. Watching this kind of nature's performance was awesome!

Texas

The Lone Star state is the second largest state in the USA. It features prairies, grasslands, forests, deserts and coastline. This rich state owes its economic boom thanks to the discovery of petroleum deposits in the 20th century. However, its traditional ranching and cowboy cultures are still preserved in various rodeo shows and horse-back ventures into the wilderness of the canyons and the desert. The bronze statue of a cowboy and a rearing horse is a tribute to Texan cowboys who tamed the American West - proudly displayed in Austin.

AMARILLO

Once Helium Capital of the World, thanks to the most productive helium fields, the city now is famous for a helicopter plant and nuclear weapons assembly and disassembly facility - the only one in the country. It is infamous for its unpredictable weather with massive temperature changes, raging winds, hailstorms, dust storms, tornadoes and floods, but offers many attractions to interested tourists.

One of them is Cadillac Ranch: an open-air installation and sculpture of 10 paint-sprayed Cadillacs (1949-1963) buried nose-first in the ground in 1974. The collection of old, used and junk cars spans the successive generations of the car line and the defining evolution of their tailfins. We arrived there before the sunrise in the misty morning. The big Texan sky was grey, and the sculpture started emerging slowly before our eyes with the mist lifting. It was an incredible view: in the middle of nowhere, we saw a line of car tails in a row sticking their boots up and all sprayed in a concoction of colours by the original artists with the tourists' added graffiti. It is actively encouraged as a public interaction with the cars - a way of expressing themselves. very hippie and very different. Well, to each their own ... Once the sun was up we could appreciate the creation in full; the photo-taking had no end ...

Then we drove towards the next state of New Mexico, stopping on the way at the Midpoint Cafe - halfway between Chicago and Los Angeles on Route 66. Its slogan states, "when you are here, you are halfway there." Indeed, the feeling was that of satisfaction and being aware that we were visiting the oldest continuously operating Route 66 cafe between Amarillo, Texas and Tucumcari, New Mexico. And it is thanks to Angel Delgadillo - still in charge and protecting the site - that this historic place has been saved for posterity with many memorabilia scattered around the area including a filling station, a Cadillac and many other motoring gadgets, as well as an ugly crust pie - baked and served as his grandma did.

New Mexico

The state's bird is the roadrunner – no wonder as the vast stretches of any land spread everywhere from the snow-capped peaks of the tip of the Rocky Mountains in the north to wide rose-coloured deserts in the south. Called the Land of Enchantment, it stands up to this distinction. Thriving on oil- drilling, cattle ranching, scientific research and arts, this place is fascinating... Not forgetting the International UFO Museum at Roswell.

TUCUMCARI

We stopped to rest at the Blue Swallow Motel – a historical rest place built in 1929 and considered the last, best and friendliest of the old-time motels. It maintains its original style with 12 units in the L-shaped building with striking neon lights, facade and a great welcoming atmosphere. Vintage memorabilia include classic cars, such as a 1963 Studebaker, and a 1956 Mercury Montclair, and a Rock-Ola jukebox in the diner. What a trip down memory lane ...

Tucumcari itself is known for its rich history, from the largest collection of pre-historic dinosaurs, to ancient Native Americans Anasazi, Comanche and Apache: from European to Mexican cultures: from the first railroad in 1902 to the birth of Route 66 in 1926 ... A very nostalgic place ...

ALBUQUERQUE

Also nicknamed Burque, it has one of the highest elevations of any large city in the USA, and it was founded in 1706 near the Rio Grande River, which is now crossed by six bridges serving the municipality. Although located in the desert, 25 per cent of the city's total area is parkland. Facebook Data Centre, Microsoft, Netflix and the International Balloon Fiesta are just a few attractions for tech buffs and adrenaline junkies.

The town is built in a traditional Spanish villa pattern; a central plaza surrounded by buildings reflecting Hispanic influence, from haciendas to restaurants. Even more historic are the basalt carvings of early Native Americans which are dated centuries ago. The place used to be a farming and shepherding community and a strategically-located trading and military outpost. Nowadays, it is a flourishing centre of the New Mexico Technology Corridor.

SANTA FE

The art cradle – the state capital founded in 1610 and known as The City Different. Located at more than 2000m above sea level is a city like no other. It is considered to have the world's largest collection of art galleries which attract international collectors and tourists. We visited some of them and the variety of styles, themes and ideas was overwhelming... Traditional, contemporary, indigenous American, Russian and Native American exhibits were everywhere, in addition to the opera, chamber music assembly, ballet, flamenco and many other artistic groups.

Legendary history and culture round every corner with visual arts, beautiful views and a home-like atmosphere. What a gem in the desert!

GALLUP

Our last stopover in New Mexico was in 200 million-year-old cliffs with the recorded presence of Anasazi, Zuni, Hopi and Navajo cultures. They have been celebrated for more than a century, during annual Inter-Tribal Indian Ceremonials. This Indian jewellery capital of the world is also home to a historical El Rancho Hotel, where people such as John Wayne, Kirk Douglas, Katherine Hepburn and Ronald Reagan used to stay while filming in the majestic scenery of New Mexico, Arizona and Utah.

Arizona

The Grand Canyon State

But not only ... We stopped on the way at the Painted Desert National Park, which encompasses the Petrified Forest. The views of layers upon layers of colourful sand deposits forming hills sculptured by the sweeping winds in changing sunlight were fantastic. But the hit of the day was awaiting after we passed the Newspaper Rock - with 650 petroglyphs etched into the boulders by people who lived there 2000 years ago. The Petrified Forest is known for its fossils and especially fallen trees that lived in the Triassic age 225 million years ago. Due to the tectonic movements of the Earth, the sediments containing the logs and examples of flora and fauna display a colourful collection of dispersed fossils forming a border between the Navajo and Apache counties.

The area is a playground for palaeontologists, who study the findings of ferns, early dinosaurs and much more on 600 archaeological sites. Photographers paradise!

FLAGSTAFF

One of America's sunniest and snowiest cities, it sits at more than 2000 metres and is surrounded by the largest ponderosa pine forests in North America.

The Dark Sky City is named so because of its low light pollution and commitment to enforcing stargazing - friendly lighting restrictions. Pluto was discovered here in 1930 in the famous observatory founded in 1894. It also served to choose the safe Moon landing sites for the Apollo missions. And the Meteor Crater - created about 50,000 years ago and featuring a squared-off outline - was used to train NASA astronauts.

Another stopover on Route 66 – this time a very brief one, as we only stayed there overnight in a lodge surrounded by the pine forest. Tempted by the fame of the place for its food and unusual waiter service, I ventured to the Black Bart's steakhouse to get us a local steak takeaway. While I was waiting for the treats I watched the waiters align in a choir and starting to sing past hits a Capella... then a pianist joined them and they continued singing, dispersing all over the saloon and taking orders – an unusual way to entertain the hungry and curious...

WILLIAMS

Also known as a gateway to the Grand Canyon National Park via the privately-owned Grand Canyon Railway. This historic Route 66 city was founded in 1881 and is still full of American-style shops and restaurants dating back to the 1900s. The Downtown District used to offer opium dens, bordellos and other rough-and-tumble attractions, but nowadays it has some kinder entertainment, reminding the tourists of the Wild West era. We were invited to a cowboy shoot out – all staged immaculately and realistically ... guns and all ...

Many places were taking us back to the roaring 50s and 60s including Pete's Gas Station Museum, full of car memorabilia and all, soda fountain, classic diners and motels.

After boarding the historic railway, we had a brief opportunity to admire the world's largest pine forests surrounding the city and famous for their varied fauna: bears, bisons, wolves living freely in these spectacular habitats. And offering limitless opportunities for outdoor enthusiasts. The final stop was in the Grand Canyon Village on the South Rim to witness two billion years of geological history in its full glory, thanks to intense sunshine and not a cloud in the sky!

THE GRAND CANYON

One of the most spectacular Wonders of the World, this gorge of the Colorado River does not cease to impress. Any time of the day and the evening. We arrived at the South Rim to enjoy a helicopter ride in the Canyon: what a flight it was! Diving past the pinnacles towards the North Rim, admiring the wind-created most amazing structures and to think that the indigenous tribes still use it as a home, living in the most inaccessible parts of the valley.

Its grandeur, sublimity and loveliness are unparalleled. Every time we have visited it, it has left us in total awe – incomparable to anything in the world.

Our next watering hole was to be found on the eastern edge of the Mojave Desert in the historic city of:

KINGMAN

The town was established in 1882 as a train stop for the Santa Fe railway. To honour its past, the Locomotive Park was established where visitors are allowed to climb and enter the exhibits, the oldest being a 1928 steam engine – the symbol of the place as the railway hub.

It is yet another Route 66 attraction, known for being a training ground for the US Army during WW2, and later for being a testing ground for the Ford and Chrysler prototypes.

It was immortalized by singer and jazz pianist Robert Troup in 1946 in his song "Get your kicks on Route 66". The city is the closest one to the Grand Canyon Skywalk – a transparent horseshoe-shaped cantilever bridge on the edge of the Grand Canyon – and a gateway to the gambling destinations in Nevada.

NEVADA

Nicknamed The Silver State, it spreads over a vast territory but is one of the least-populated states. Its economy is mostly based on mining gold and silver and tourism. Three-quarters of the population lives in the metropolitan area of Las Vegas - the cultural, financial and commercial centre of Nevada, in a basin on the floor of the Mojave Desert.

LAS VEGAS or THE MEADOWS

The world centre of adult entertainment gained its nickname Sin City in 1930, being the only place allowing gambling in the States. It thrived even more thanks to the construction of the nearby Hoover Dam. After WW2, its famous Strip was filled with lavishly decorated themed casinos, hotels and big-name entertainment.

In the 50s the city was nicknamed Atomic City, as the Nevada Test Site was used to test atomic explosions. The residents and visitors were witn essing large mushrooms, and were exposed to the fallout for over a decade.

Most casinos are located downtown on Fremont Street, named after its founder, the oldest being the Golden Gate Casino, built in 1906. Another one, The Golden Nugget, still the symbol of the gambling enthusiasts, was our adobe for two nights. We hoped to enjoy a night walk along the street and down the Strip, but were overwhelmed by the crowd milling on the pedestrian passage ... quick decision to return to our room and leave the fun for the next day.

The Strip is considered one of the most popular and iconic tourist destinations in the world, with its contemporary architecture, lights and a variety of attractions. Ceasar's Palace with its Roman decor and the replica of the Trevi fountain and many historical symbols of Rome, the Flamingo, and its famous star shows, the MGM with its lion guarding the entrance, the New York, New York with a rollercoaster, the Luxor welcoming the gamblers with the replica of Sphynx, the Bellagio with its spectacular fountain displays dancing to music and Paris with the Montgolfier brothers' balloon replica marking the place. Not forgetting the Venetian, the Wynn, and the Encore resorts. As the weather can be oppressive, there are sprinklers distributed along the Strip to cool down the gambling fans.

The recent addition to the collection was the Strat Hotel, Casino and SkyPod with its famous Stratosphere tower and the Big Shot gravity drop attraction accelerating to 4G, and the Thrill ride 300m above the ground. The High Roller - the highest rollercoaster in the world - was dismantled, as it failed to provide the expected adrenaline rushes...

This Marriage Capital of the World offers licenses – provided you have the necessary documents and $77 – within minutes every day until midnight. The wedding chapels are scattered along the Strip and offer themed weddings: from Fairy Tale, Halloween and Hawaiian, to Star Trek, Star War and Elvis and Michael Jackson impersonators. The kitsch rules are in tune with many other displays of local attractions.

From Las Vegas, passing the newly constructed complexes, including the Trump Tower clad in gold and looking omnipotent in the rising sunlight, we drove southwest on to the last state of our adventure.

California

The Golden State deserves its nickname. Its glorious history can be traced in every region from the Mojave Desert and its Calico Ghost town, reminding us of the old West silver mining days, to the Sierra Nevada Mountains and the Central Valley farmlands covered with vineyards and redwood forests.

The Gold Rush in the late 1880s started its prosperity, and it continues to this day as the global trendsetter in entertainment in Los Angeles, technology in San Francisco - where the hippie counterculture started, and it continues its beach and car trend - together with the communication innovation of the internet and the personal computer. On its Pacific coast, it is covered with 900 miles of cliff-lined beaches, and is famous for its scenic landscape.

We reached Santa Monica in the late afternoon, and completing the Route 66 challenge - we reached the end of the trail. The local hotel was a well- deserved resting place, and we had a chance to visit Venice Beach with its training grounds, skaters park, and fascinating array of all styles of residences. Then we went on the paddling boat and visited the bay, and finally the certificates and farewells.

It was intense, full of climate changes, new experiences, full of history and human strife. We did it on the luxury coach ... they did it in horse-drawn wagons ... we did it in peace ... they did it in wild western conditions ... We were welcomed ... they were invaders... but it was worth it! In every way! We were exhausted by being so happy to have followed the Mother Road - the road to riches of the continent, still there for grabs, whatever you fancy...

The place is a hotchpotch of cultures old and new, nations from every possible corner of the world, all religious representations, every language imaginable and every skin shade under the sun ... They all live together, contributing to the cosmopolitan character of the place and enriching its success with varying respect for each other and its history.

Quite an experience spending all this time in such a vast country and learning so much ... The present American dream cost them a lot of sacrifices, struggle and not-so-honourable dealings with the rightful owners of the land - the indigenous people who are still there, slowly reclaiming their rights and recognition.

CHAPTER 15

BACK HOME...

Roystonian beauty...

The weather welcome was as usual: from the cloudless skies of the Western Coast of the USA to the grey skies of the English islands. Hardly surprising, as the place is exposed to six different weather currents, and one never knows which season is coming tomorrow! Although recently, the summers have become very hot and dry, and the rains often resemble monsoons ... causing frightening flooding and destruction. There is also a widespread problem of land erosion, as the sea is mercilessly reclaiming the land, much to everybody's despair. The collapsed houses are a grim reminder of nature's power - human resourcefulness to tame it is failing on a yearly basis ...

It took us a while to recover from our American adventure, and life followed its traditional path.

I continued with my interpreting assignments having to support the incoming Polish arrivals flocking to the UK in their droves: all social types of all professions and many without any idea for life. It was very interesting to observe the newcomers with their families in their council houses expecting to be provided with everything, including the obvious benefits. On my arrival, there was no support offered in any shape or form, not to mention that we were not allowed to work! It was all purely political as we came from the opposite bloc and were not considered equally worthy of the consideration of the hosts. This situation led to developing the manoeuvring skills to avoid the strict regulations of the state. Many shared accommodation and many a night was spent on the airbed on the floor in a friend's rented room. Many of my friends used to work and share jobs and the grey zone was thriving ... Those were the challenging young times and taught us a lot about political injustices, social inequalities and the ways to survive in a capitalistic society.

The recent influx of our compatriots has not had such experiences as, per the EU rules, they were entitled to everything as European citizens – without contributing to the taxpayers' coffers as we had to.

Many spoke English and had no issues establishing successfully in their firms and companies. But there was a large percentage of them who came without any language, occupation nor a plan for the future. I was called to courts, schools, surgeries and hospitals, helping them to communicate and integrate into the new society.

Much to my dismay, I faced many barriers and a reluctance to do so. Even free English lessons I offered locally with a grant from the local council had to be abandoned as there were very few takers. And it was very disappointing to someone who came here decades ago and had to start from zero without any support.

Both Caroline and Sophie caught the travelling bug. Caroline continued her far-away conquests and lived for a while in Thailand. After the great experiment, she returned to Cambridge and started her work in the computer industry, occasionally having a break abroad all over the world.

Sophie settled in Royston. She finished her new course in nursing and thrived as a community nurse. Her escapes were closer to home. She also married and then divorced her husband a couple of years later. Her new partner Mark and their rescue greyhound live together in a house on the hill close to beautiful woods and fields spreading far past the town, and giving so much pleasure to the locals and their pooches. Emma returned to her creative work at Rowan art studio and continued volunteering in the local nursery, much to her and their delight.

Her art studio was taking part in many exhibitions in Cambridge and elsewhere. One of them was a photography contest called Snap and my picture of her - during the Aerosmith concert in Hyde Park singing in ecstasy in the pouring rain - won a distinction. The photo was enlarged and placed on a huge cube with other winners, and was sent as an exhibition of special needs successes round the country.

The awards were given at the Camden Studio by EastEnders' actors. Her favourite was John Altman, who played Nick Cotton in the series. Her delight to see him and shake his hand was the pick of the day! And they met again some years ago at the Stevenage theatre, where he played Aladdin, and invited her to his dressing room. The encounter was a very happy occasion for both – the souvenir photo taken says it all!

My life followed a routine path and I continued to be a mother, a carer, a taxi driver and a cook. Professionally, I focused on the linguistic side of my career. Having been invited to run some evening Spanish classes, I jumped at the idea, as it took me back to my university years. All 10 participants were very enthusiastic and of varying levels of Spanish language knowledge. From complete beginners to fluent poetry reciters - quite a challenging mixture. We stayed together for two years and had real fun learning the secrets of this beautiful and romantic language of Don Quijote.

I was asked to run a Polish course. We started with 10 students of varying backgrounds and completed the yearly programme with four. The complexity and grammar proved too much for most... My Polish course times sprang to mind when I was a correspondence tutor. Much to my surprise, I was informed by one of my students, who was a neurosurgeon, that he was giving up the challenge and returning to his profession - why wasn't I surprised?

We continued enjoying our outings, London visits, theatre, and concerts. Especially the ones in the open air in Hyde Park and in other parts of the country. Emma was hooked on Aerosmith, so we saw them twice in different locations - the smiles on her face stayed there for a long time. All birthday celebrations were also marked with special meals out and visits from local ice-skating to the Harry Potter Experience and more, in London.

EMMA'S SPECIAL BIRTHDAY TRIP

Wow! What a Week!

Considering decades of check-ups, hospital visits and reviews, Emma's health was stable and her prognosis was very good. In fact, she was doing so well that we were able to travel the world and enjoy its marvels without any obstacles. So, for her 35th birthday, she was given a choice of treats, and she chose the 80s music cruise -her favourite music period as she was born in the 80s - sailing from her beloved America!

The expectations were high, the anticipation even higher, as we flew to Ft. Lauderdale. The shock of arriving in February from cold and grey England to scorching heat in Florida was bad enough, but to be welcomed by a monsoon at night was another story ... We stayed for a couple of nights in The Chocolate Hotel, which turned out to be a local hub for ex-hippies, hobos and other unusual characters. We had to share a flat with some obscure chap who rented a room in our flat and could not do anything about it as the rest of the hotel was full. The decor was putting us in the right mood for the cruise, all as if teletransported from the 70s, including the beds and linen. The flower power atmosphere was somewhat strange, possibly because we had never experienced such surroundings in the past ... You learn every day ... and the lesson turned out to be a very positive one.

We reached the port and went through the embarkation process. The mood of the 80s was everywhere. People were wearing colourful costumes, the music was taking us back to my youth and everyone was smiling! Apparently, the amount of luggage per passenger for this cruise was among the highest of the year. Emma hastily studied the programme and started talking about the bands scheduled to take us back to the 80s every day on the ship.

Jefferson Starship, famous for "We Built This City", Berlin for "Take My Breath Away", Tiffany for "I Think We're Alone Now", Cutting Crew for "I Just Died In Your Arms Tonight", Club Nouveau for "Lean On Me" and Jessie's Girl – the 80s tribute band which covers the hits of this amazing decade every Saturday night at the Le Poisson Rouge in Greenwich Village in New York – just to name a few!

Every night was a different theme night: from Back to the 80s, Enchantment Under the Sea, Neon Mardi Gras Party, Nightmare on the 80s Cruise, Pop Icon night to Later Dude, See Ya Next Year ... No wonder they brought so many cases on board.

We were not aware that it was the fourth consecutive sailing of this type, and many people knew each other from previous years; hence the atmosphere was so friendly and cool; many shared their paraphernalia with others, and many a time, we came back to our cabin with rows of beads, bracelets, and flowers. Emma was also celebrated by the crew with a special birthday card and some cruise presents.

We sailed south from the very modern and progressive port - close to the famous swamps of the Everglade, full of infamous alligators - through the Caribbean Sea, the Bahamas and with music on full blast! The next day was a day at sea, and we had a chance to explore the ship and the venues for endless music events. Everywhere there were banners, posters and decorations in psychedelic colours, making you smile and reminisce... passengers wearing the 80s stuff and reliving their youth...

The first stop was on Cozumel – a limestone island off the coast of the Mexican inland and ranked the world's premier fishing and diving ground. And a mere ferry ride away we could explore centuries of human splendour in the Mayan ruins at Tulum, spectacularly sited on the sea cliffs. All day we enjoyed the views, sea and local history.

And we continued the next day at Puerto Costa Maya port on the Yucatan Peninsula with a visit to beautifully preserved Mayan temples. That was followed by contrast with yet another evening concert in the main hall – we were getting in the right state of mind...

Belize (old British Honduras granted independence in 1981 -another 80s addition) - the only English-speaking country in Central America -– welcomed us with a local dance show and cheered for Poland when we mentioned my origins. A little moving gesture adding to our elevated moods. We went on an airboat in the local swamps and tried to find some unusual indigenous creatures to no effect! It was as if a magic wand hid all local creatures, great and small, away from the intruding tourists! But at least the driver managed to show off his professional skills, zooming through the water at high speed and performing the most dramatic turns... an exhilarating experience!

This second-largest reef system in the world is an incredible spot for snorkelling and diving. It is also famous for its biodiversity and ecotourism with excursions available into the unspoilt tropical rainforest, wildlife reserves and multiple cave systems. It delivers great memories, whether you choose water, beach, or jungle. And it also has many Mayan sites worth a visit.

However, a day there can only allow some treats - next time, perhaps?

We passed on the evening scary theme and the Zombie Pub trail and the Scream Queen competition, enjoying the usual evening walk on the deck and finally chilling on the balcony watching the stars and the waves on our way back north - nature's therapy at its best!

The last stop was at Key West Island near Florida – the most southernmost point of the USA, accessible from the mainland via the Overseas Highway. Its climate and waters have been an attraction for centuries. Only 90 miles from Cuba, and famous for its pastel-hued conch-style architecture. Its main street - Duval Street - is an energetic strip buzzing with tourists, nightlife and many attractions, including Ernest Hemingway's waterhole Sloopy Joe's. In fact, rum, hammocks and Cuban food are the basis of its idle- paced city. The last one in our itinerary...

Having disembarked in Fort Lauderdale, we headed for the airport to fly to Emma's final choice of destination: Washington. She has always had a soft spot for Donald Trump and wanted to see where he lived!

Why not? We were over the pond anyway, so it was a perfect end to our buzzing trip!

We stayed in a traditional motel on the outskirts of the city and enjoyed the surroundings: classic American detached houses lining the streets, each with a front, and many marked with patriotic flags and God bless America- type slogans. There was a definite community spirit there, marked further by a freely accessible cabinet full of books to borrow/share - what a lovely recycling idea!

We had to visit the sights - down my memory lane - and decided to do it our way using public transport. The first stop was the White House - as white as it could be, and guarded by a flank of policemen armed up to the teeth and keeping the tourists and the protesters a safe distance from the iron fence surrounding the grounds. The high level of security did not deter the demonstrators from carrying placards with texts varying from polite to obscene and all referring to Trump.

Emma was very excited, as every now and then a government car drove through going to the side gates - she hoped to see him. But it was not to be...

The walk to the National Mall took us past the stands with all the souvenir paraphernalia: everything one can imagine bearing his picture or name or the MAGA slogan insisting on Making America Great Again. He hoped...

The Mall is a landscaped park full of interesting historical buildings and monuments from the Capitol to Washington's

Monument and the Lincoln Memorial running along the Potomac River.

The weather was beautiful and the Reflecting Pool provided an additional attraction: the reflection of Washington's Obelisk – the world's tallest stone structure - commemorating him as a commander in the Revolutionary War and the First American president. Rising proudly between the Capitol - the neoclassic building erected in the 1800s - and the Lincoln Memorial, a colossal marble figure sitting in a temple-like construction reminding all of his role in the Civil War, abolishing slavery and rising from the national crisis by modernizing American economy before his assassination in 1865.

The next day we visited the Pentagon and Arlington Cemetery Day, both reflecting events which we witnessed in modern times. The Memorial in the Pentagon to the victims of the 9/11 attack is very moving: a combination of simple illuminated benches - 184 of them dedicated to those who died in the building, and those who died on the plane. A very quiet and solemn place surrounded by an ascending wall signifying the ages of the terror victims, from three to 71. And many trees offering shade and time for reflection...

The mood continued at the Arlington National Cemetery, the largest military cemetery, where the dead of the nation's conflicts from the Civil War to modern times are buried.

We walked for miles in the vast undulating area, looking at the headstones with markings of all religions and reminding us of the futility of it all. In my memory the Korean, Vietnamese and more recent conflicts are still vivid; as well as incidents such as the visit to JF Kennedy's grave was very emotional. We stood there watching the eternal flame for ages ... the simplicity of the grave and total silence surrounding the place were overwhelming and the consequences of the act truly so...

Miles and miles of varying groups of gravestones, reminding all of the pain and grief of millions affected by the greed and strife for power ... and at what cost...

But everything has to come to an end. We left Washington the next day, full of new experiences and lessons in local geography, politics and history.

Back home, it took us a while to recover from the obvious jetlag! But the music overload, new memories and famous sights are still with us, and waiting to be repeated.

CHAPTER 16

MAKING CINEMATOGRAPHIC RIPPLES IN MEXICO

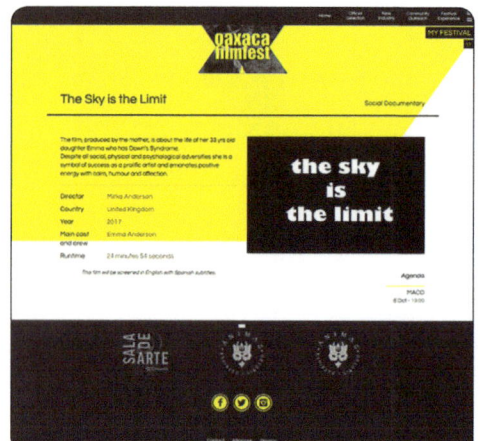

It is official - we are in!

To spread the word to a larger audience - the world - about my mission via the documentary, I joined an agency in Canada called Filmfreeway, which keeps an eye on all film festivals. It informs all interested in future film celebrations on all continents in a weekly bulletin and allows the film community to submit its films with a fee to the selected ones. It also informs of rejections, selections and final awards in recognition of the films in any category.

We managed to amass 50 awards in many categories in various corners of the world, from Hawaii to Bhutan. The first one came from Chile for the best director, then Venezuela for special and Mexico for the best documentary. This was followed by the best documentary recognized in Delaware, Kentucky, New Mexico, California (LA and Hollywood), Hawaii, New York City and the Channel Islands. European festivals appreciated our film in Spain, Turkey, Belgium, France, England, Scotland, Russia and Poland. Asia also rewarded us with prizes in the Philippines, Bali, India, Goa, Bhutan and Indonesia for human rights. Also, Canada and New Zealand.

To top it, the news came from our submitter that my documentary was going to be screened in front of a live audience in Mexico at the Oaxaca Film Festival!

I was very excited as my mission was progressing steadily and reaching wider and wider audiences. But to face the audience and respond to them in a Q&A session - that took my experience to yet another level!

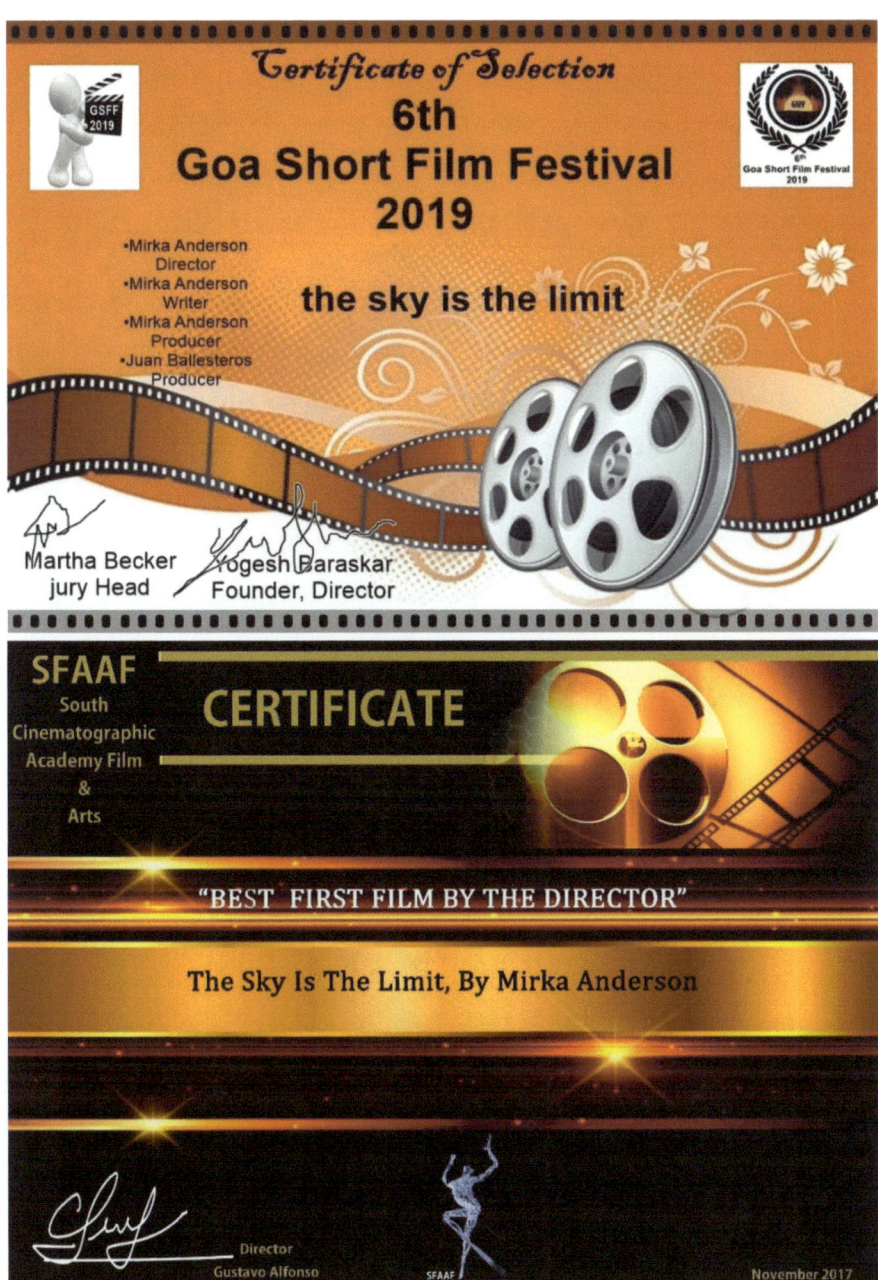

LA – HERE WE COME AGAIN!

With the tickets booked and smiles on our faces, we ventured out to conquer - yet again - North America. The first stopover was in Los Angeles, where we did our down-the-memory-lane Downtown and Hollywood ... Not much change from the previous visit, apart from some additional stars on the Walk of Fame pavement.

Emma found the star of her favourite Donald Trump and Aerosmith and met the Marvel characters with the compulsory photo which had to be taken with Spiderman! And tourists and souvenir shops everywhere. In one of them, she disappeared momentarily and made me worried but soon emerged from the Oscar statuettes section with a medium-sized one marked The Best Mum announcing that it was my early birthday present! What a star!

MEXICAN VIBES...

We flew to Oaxaca (pronounced wahaka) via Mexico City and landed there in the middle of the night in pouring rain. We were transferred by the festival organisers to our hotel called One in the old part of this UNESCO World Heritage Site since 1987. It was a modern basic hotel full of festival attendees.

In the morning, we woke up to a panoramic view overlooking the mountain range of the Sierra Madre, shrouded in fog and be coning with its stunning flora and fauna. And local Zapotecs - "The True People" who started the settlement in 2000 BC - and Mixtecs "The Place of the Cloud People" still inhabiting and thriving in their land. The place was first discovered in the late 1500s by Spaniards accompanied by Aztecs who came here as gold prospectors. Many a building reminds the visitor of its past colonial glory: the Cathedral, the Monastery, and the Zocalo park with its classic bandstand, all in Spanish and Moorish styles, renovated and accessible to visit bearing marks of previous earthquakes and time ... And being particularly prone to seismic activity in Mexico, it does suffer strong ones as the country is located in a subduction zone: an oceanic plate - the Cocos - is gradually sinking beneath a continental plate - the North American.

The main street is cobbled with local stone and runs along colourful single- storey buildings converted into cafes and art shops. It took us to the street vendor of the local delicacy *tejate* – a non-alcoholic drink made with maize and cocoa dating back to pre-Hispanic times. Delicious! After refreshments, we continued to walk towards the Town Hall where the screening of our documentary was to happen. From a distance, we were treated to a real Mexican music concert which included the guitar-like six-string instrument, the salterio – a five-box cymbal-like metal stringed instrument played by plucking the strings with a metal pick - and the trumpet – a must in any Mexican ensemble. The atmosphere was happy-go-lucky and we nearly missed our scheduled screening ...

LIVE AUDIENCE EXPERIENCE

The Town Hall, built in classical Spanish style, with its wide marble staircase and walls decorated with portraits of local achievers, was grandiose. We walked up to the projection rooms and found our audience. The documentary was one of four screened in the same group, followed by the Q and A session. Emma was very excited and really overwhelmed by the experience - so much so, that after the screening she did not want to join me to face the audience, and I had to answer the queries on my own. The star of the show remained in the shadows of fame!

The afternoon proved to be very emotional. The questions showed real interest in the subject matter, and my director's ego was growing...

The closing ceremony was very informal and gave us the opportunity to meet many local and foreign filmmakers and people of interest in the industry. All is well that ends well - and it seriously did, with spectacular views over this historic town bathed in streetlights and a very special atmosphere! Thank you, Oaxaca, for your welcome and recognition!

CUBAN STOP-OVER

To recover from all these new stimuli and enjoy a well-deserved break: where else but in Havana? Our memories from previous visits were so vivid that a week in the Hemingway Marina seemed a nice change from the cold climate in Mexico. The hotel we booked looked good in the brochure, but Cuban reality hit us hard ...

The whole complex was badly run and maintained. There were cockroaches - apparently, a good sign, as these creatures favour clean places - and broken plaster on the outside walls. The swimming pool had not been looked after and had many dangerously broken elements. The dining area left a lot to be desired: the chairs looked painted white with pieces of dried food on them, and the bar stank of many unpleasant things.

The bedroom was spacious and overlooked the canal - just as the writer planned it. But wherever we walked, there were electrical wires sticking out of the ground! Having spoken to the staff, it became clear that the place was run by an incompetent manager and it was a place for distinguished Communist party members and their families! All guests were Cuban - we were the only foreigners! My childhood flashed before my eyes, remembering similar holiday camps reserved for the loyal party's elite ... But in a much better state of repair.

As the visit was short, and the area was very quiet with the marina full of all kinds of yachts from all over the world - the fees for mooring were negligible - we had a unique chance to admire many super attractive vessels first-hand; the sunsets were also unforgettable ...

And the re-visit to Havana - which this time we reached by speedboat. The guys were not in much hurry as on the way they tried to catch their dinner – fishing while we sailed and involving Emma – much to her content, as she has never fished for a big one before.

Havana - as usual, was bustling with life: buses, people and a collection of the old Cadillacs, Oldsmobile, Pontiacs and Fords, all painstakingly restored and shining in the sun with all colours of the palette, next to traditional horse-driven coaches offering a ride in the old style. From the Town Hall – which is a replica of the Capitol in Washington – we drove to Independence Square, which reminds everyone that Che Guevarra and Castro made this country as it is now - their stylized metal head portraits adorn the place.

Passing through the city we admired the beautiful trees abundant with spectacular arrays of flowers, the colourful buildings, and finally, the central passage leading the harbour - listed by UNESCO and lined with colonial and post-colonial architectural gems - many in a very sorry state, but slowly being restored to their previous glory. Great place with a great atmosphere!

The airport transport was a real surprise. We travelled in a 50-year-old Daimler – green outside and inside, with its comfortably padded seats and the space of a good-sized study.

Sheer luxury! And after a final cup of genuine Cuban coffee - the best I have ever tasted - we waved goodbye to this beautiful and colourful island bathed in exotic plants and flowers, and run in the old-fashioned controlling dictatorship ... with images of Castro's and Che Gevara's heads appearing here and there to remind all about their grandiosity and - for those more tuned in historically - their oppressive and restrictive ideology.

This system has ruled in this country for more than seven decades and has defied all attempts to bring the system down. Even the Bay of the Pigs conflict in the 60s.

The Old Town in Havana is full of cigar-smoking old ladies dressed in traditional costumes, reminding the tourists of their best export product - cigars. And the old cars refurbished to the highest of standards are a reminder of the "good old days" of wealthy capitalist visitors - including Hemingway and Sinatra - who added to Havana's fame with their famous and not-so-famous works.

Finally, Cubans praise themselves for being the nation leading in educational standards in medicine. Their doctors are claimed to be the best in the world.

CHAPTER 17

TIME FLIES ...

1973 - 2021

Five decades of life-learning curve have passed: from the middle of the Socialist Bloc to the centre of capitalist Europe has been an unexpectedly amazing experience with its ups and downs, cultural challenges, mentality shocks and new pastures altogether in the new land, new culture and new history outlooks.

The curve is very sinusoidal. The initial excitement about arranging and executing my dream trip to England, and having to learn to jump over the red tape, and the general misleading attitude towards the "rotten" West, but also manipulating the status quo in Poland by planning the departure straight after graduation to avoid a compulsory work placement assigned ad hoc by the socialist employment system.

In addition, the British Consulate requirements had to be satisfied to ensure a smooth entry into the country. The official invitation from a sponsor was a must and a letter of assurance of accommodation allocation and financial support was also needed. These were arranged between families and friends to help us youngsters to have a taste of life over there. The system worked very well and, in case a dissatisfied newcomer was unhappy with the conditions, there was always a chance to change them - we lived in a free world!

Once we had flown into Heathrow - with the total sum of £4.65 allowed officially by the Polish Government in their restrictive/ humiliating move to limit the outflow of foreign currency from the state coffers - reality struck hard!

England was welcoming, with smiles even on the immigration officer's face. All was new, and many things were curious like the unknown fact that steak is cut with a steak knife! And fish with a fish knife! The list is endless yet educational, and the feeling of being able to see and experience all these intricacies in our common European culture was fascinating. Also, the fact that we could actually visit the historical sites and buildings and witness historical events we had only read about in our language books for decades was exhilarating.

However, in those days, we had no work permits and were forced to join the grey market. Many cash-in-hand jobs were then available, so we worked everywhere we could from Wimpy's to cleaning hotels, houses and whatever we could. There was a great sense of camaraderie: we helped each other, be it with lodgings (sleeping on the floor in someone's room) or with work: sharing, recommending and organising meetings.

Every six months, we had to face the purely bureaucratic demand of the Home Office to extend our visitor visa. It involved travelling to Croydon with our passports and the proof that we were working on integrating into society by improving our English. As we spoke it quite well, we decided to use our initiative and enrol at UCL on the English course for foreigners. It was the easiest solution and did not collide with our social and working arrangements.

Time flew by and after two years of this extraordinary "holiday", a great life decision was to be made regarding the future. As the Polish passports were not renewable and valid only for two years, we had to consider various options. Some decided to go back home, some moved on to the continental West, and some got married, with varying success...

I married my Englishman -– or to be precise, a Geordie man - and having been granted citizenship, started to live a normal as normal life can be. First, I got my proper job in an insurance company near Fleet Street - then the centre of journalism - and using a typewriter, spent hours writing letters to the customers reminding them of approaching renewal dates. This first- hand experience of working in an office as a team member was invaluable and proved that not all that shines is gold ... especially narcissistic bosses...

We lived in Bayswater at the time, next to Hyde Park, which was a lifesaver when my firstborn arrived. Caroline was a fast developer and a very inquisitive little lady, who joined the local nursery at the age of four much to her and their delight. And mine, as I was offered a place on the full-time speech therapy course at the School of the Study in Human Communication in Waterloo. It was an incredible event in my life as my interview with director Margaret Fawcett lasted half an hour, and afterwards I received a phone call, was offered a place and allowed to do three years in two, taking into consideration the subjects I took at Warsaw University.

I was stunned: no documents were presented, no certificates were demanded - total trust and confidence in my suitability. Coming from a country where all achievements had to be documented, verified and filed before even being invited to an interview attended by many academics - that was unbelievable! My major chance for professional success was given to me in spite of the general attitude to foreigners and their different accents. Make it or break it! The choice was mine. I did make it, and after two years of hard work and sacrifices I was granted a diploma in speech therapy - the only Pole in a very English profession...

Later I spread my linguistic wings and was involved in the creation of the Polish language course, which was published with great pomp by the Linguaphone Institute in London. This experience and consequent responsibility of guiding the correspondence students through the grammatical jungle of the Polish tongue was totally new and threw light upon its complexity, both in grammar and articulation structures. But many made it, and the satisfaction was really enormous!

And then came the decision of a lifetime: travelling around the world with a one-year stop-over in New Zealand. It took us one-and-a-half months to reach Auckland visiting Sri Lanka, Indonesia, Singapore and Australia on the way. New climates, races, cultures, cuisines, landscapes and colours ... everywhere ... bathed in permanent sunshine and an occasional monsoon, always vibrant and attractive, even through the sheets of rainfall pouring from the sky.

Auckland was welcoming with its famous daily attractions of possible yachting in the morning and skiing on Mt. Ruapehu in the afternoon. My professional skills were gradually improving in the North Shore Waitakere Hospitals. The trips outside this hilly giant took us to volcanic Rotorua, the glow worm caves and prehistoric fern forests in search of a kiwi - the symbol of the place - but no luck.

A year later, on the way back to the UK, we stopped in the remote Polynesian Archipelago and admired the calm and serenity of the place. Finally, it was back to our civilisation: with its skyscrapers, motorways and abundance of everything from space, houses, cars, goods and food to crime, illegal migration and social frictions. We were back in western reality in the USA. A giant of a country, with vast areas of interest, including canyons, deserts, and historical sites of importance reflecting the country's turbulent past and present history.

A hotchpotch of world cultures and traditions living together in apparent unison and benefiting from a multitude of different mentalities and approaches to lifestyles: from the simple-living Amish community to the money-chasing bankers in Wall Street, and from the sandy beaches of California to the alligator-ridden Everglades in Florida. The land of extreme and unique flora and fauna, from indigenous Joshua trees to the most popular maples.

The land of varying landscapes from the snowy Rockies to the Great Plains. And extreme climatic zones, from the coldest Alaska to scorching Hawaii. This fascinating land enchanted us for four months while we were traversing it in our camper on our way back home ...

We arrived in London after two days of sleeping at JFK in New York in our rented limousine due to the extreme holiday traffic on Independence Day.

Back home was not as happy as it seemed. Initially, I had to approach my friend in Chelsea to let us stay with her, but it did not last long – my dear husband was celebrating our return too eagerly and his return in the middle of the night in an intoxicated state became a nuisance. So we had to leave and move to Enfield in north London - his old Geordie friends were very accepting and tolerant -yet another lesson that there still are some kind people who are willing to help and offer support in times of need.

I decided to visit Poland as travelling was allowed following a period of prohibition after the state of emergency was declared due to the anti- government activity by Solidarnosc workers' movement.

My husband stayed to look for suitable accommodation for us in the area as we could not afford any property in London following the economic boom during our absence. Caroline and I left for Warsaw, and a month later, I discovered I was pregnant, much to my delight!

The house we bought was located in a small village. Emma was born with the unexpected condition of Down Syndrome. My life axis flipped 180 degrees. Mother Nature proved yet again who is in charge ... Although I was familiar with the condition as a student, I was totally taken aback by the consultant paediatrician's announcement that "you don't have to take her home – she won't do anything anyway" - the caring profession's attitude? That and the later discovered fact of gross medical negligence as we were discharged a week later without any thorough examination.

The result was a very unhappy discovery nine months later of a hole in Emma's heart – reconstructed and still working after decades since the operation. A lesson in humility, patience and hope.

Life and strife went on with all its rises and falls. The biggest one came a year after Sophie was born. Overwhelmed by parenting responsibilities, I trusted that my husband's plans to build a large house in the village would come true, knowing he employed a group of specialists to guide his venture - much to my total disappointment. The end result was a disaster. The bank took over both properties to cover the loan, and we were left homeless.

The feeling of all being lost while standing in the street with three daughters was dreadful. Had it happened somewhere else, I would have panicked. But fortunately, the local council stepped in and allocated us a bungalow in an adjacent village as temporary accommodation. The relief was indescribable... and peace of mind and soul endured.

Curtsying in front of Anne, Princess Royal - the Chancellor of The University of London.

That was followed by another unique and positive experience in The Royal Albert Hall. All graduates and post-graduates from University College, London, were given their certificates in a ceremony hosted by the Chancellor Princess Anne. With all the royal pomp and decorum, it was a day to always remember. The auditorium full of students from all over the world lining up to curtsy in front of the royal - the fact snapped by the camera taking a picture for posterity - quite an occasion to feel special and proud! The pictures after were individual photos with the triumphant degree bearers holding the sacred piece of paper - mine being a MSC in human communication.

After a fairly straightforward divorce, which again gave me another lesson in English patriarchal social structure and the privileges which come with it, the family started a new chapter in our history. Just the four of us continued, happily adjusting to the new reality and following individual life routes. Caroline continued at a private school in Cambridge, Emma attended a local school in the village and Sophie joined a playgroup. After-school activities also took up a lot of time, from dance lessons and horse-riding to gymnastics and instrument learning sessions. Life was busy and very active.

A year later, we were offered a semi-detached house in Bassingbourn - we were going back to our roots! The place was newly built, spacious and very safe as it was in a cul-de-sac. The neighbours had three children, so there was instant company to play with – smiles all the way!

My parents came to visit for a month or so, adding to our family life with new ideas and trips in England and abroad. As their father's family contacts were non-existent, it was very important to maintain the Polish links for many reasons. Caroline could speak Polish and had a GCSE in it, Emma was picking up some words and phrases and Sophie followed suit. Other members of the family also came round and made the girls feel a part of the clan.

We also visited them regularly and spent many summers enjoying the lake district, the mountains and many places around and in Warsaw itself. All memories were very positive and full of fun. And our travels abroad never ceased - every year or twice a year, we ventured to Europe and even further, including Thailand where Caroline moved with her boyfriend, and we joined them for a couple of Christmases.

I continued working, and after 17 years of a fascinating and very educational professional experience, decided to retire and focus on my linguistic hobbies – namely interpreting. The clients were so varied in need of support, that I a had a chance to study the social aspect of newcomers from Spain and Poland. The issues they faced in the new environment were challenging and a lot of reassuring and advisory input was needed to put them at ease, and help them to assimilate the new pastures. Some cases were insurmountable, and many complicated problems had to be resolved with respective government agencies, or they had to be simply guided to consider returning to their native land.

Another challenge was my idea of setting up a Polish grocery store in Royston town in the main square. The location was perfect, and a large range of satisfied clientele used to visit us regularly ... but our downfall was a lack of cooperation from the suppliers: never on time and missing deadlines. The venture had to close - much to everyone's disappointment.

The failure was compensated by the move to a flat in Royston, which made me very happy: we were close to the station, so my admired London was easily accessible. Emma's taxis to Cambridge were local and Sophie's school bus was picking her up from the bus stop opposite our building. The communal gardens were maintained by a professional gardener, the staircase was cleaned regularly by an employed cleaner and the only thing to take care of was our flat - what a relief to a not-very-domesticated mother!

And so it went - all those years lived to the full and gone - shame so quickly. But age is no obstacle to the adventurous soul ...

However, life events never cease to surprise ... after 70 years of my stay on this planet, my enthusiasm for learning the new and exploring the world was suddenly muted. The pandemic turned our lives, dreams, expectations and plans upside down. Suddenly, we became prisoners in our own houses. The country went into a lockdown. Emma and I had to shield ourselves for a year because of her suppressed immune system and I had to join her because my age group was deemed very vulnerable. The media went into a state of frenzy: every day we had graphs displayed with data about the numbers of infections and deaths and hospital admissions. Special applications on mobile phones were installed and the public was advised to register on them. Shopping was done over the internet and delivered by respective supermarkets and family and friends. Emma's studio set up activity sessions on the computer via Zoom. We felt paralysed and dismayed by the situation. Covid 19 conquered the world ...

It was 18 months of protection in every sense of the word, one big unknown and desperate race of the wealthy countries to find an effective vaccine. And then the money-spinning propaganda started praising some and rejecting others as less effective. The conspiracy theorists were taking over social media, disclosing the corrupt moves of various governments, misleading science-based information and calling for some rebellious anti- vaccine demonstrations.

Indeed, there were lots of cases of misrepresentation of facts, giving contracts to family and friends, and mismanagement of public funds, which are being investigated by the Parliamentary Commissions. But the worst was the feeling of helplessness.

Although the situation has improved after 80 per cent of the population was vaccinated and our restrictions have been lifted, so there is a choice in wearing a mask or shopping as before, but the overall mood is low. With the number of infections rising again and daily death numbers increasing steadily. we might be forced into another isolation phase ... What a bizarre reality we are living in.

At least, the borders have been opened and we managed to fly to Madeira for a week.

The complete change of environment, air and atmosphere were the best antidote for our subdued faces: we enjoyed the place, its people, food, sights and attention to cleanliness. And we managed to see the local annual flower festival preparations - including flower carpets and floats with beautiful ladies adorning them in their spectacularly elegant dresses.

And very soon after, we were off to celebrate my 70th birthday in Paris, including a two-day visit to Disneyland, where one forgets about the problems and age and joins in the fun and fesitivities without any reservations! Something for the body and the soul ...

My Snow White dress is ready and I will enjoy my visit in the park as a vintage Snow White, although she has reached the ripe age of 84 by now ...

CHAPTER 18

AND FINALLY...

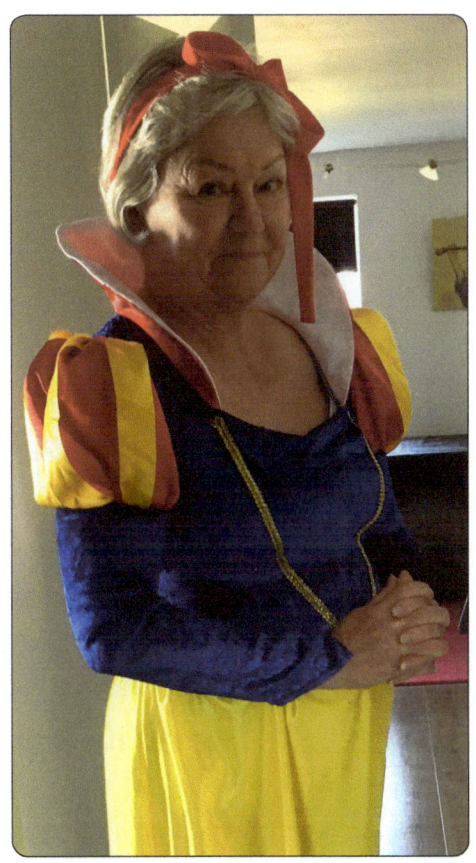

Getting in the mood ... for my 70s celebration

The down-the-memory lane trip to Paris. Having taken the children to Disneyland 23 years ago, it was time to reverse the roles. Sophie organized mum's whim and made it a great success. After two years of restrictions and general negativity and uncertainty, we escaped to the Continent via Eurostar from St. Pancras Station in London. Travelling under the Channel at 334.7 km/hour and not feeling a single bump was incredible... Arriving at Disneyland hotel Cheyenne - named so after the indigenous people of the Great Plains in the USA - in the middle of the night was another illuminated treat. The theme of the hotel was Toy Story and we stayed in the western-style room decorated with wallpaper with Woody and Jessica on it ... Yee- haw!

And then the cake arrived with 70 candles and a bottle of champagne! Let the celebrations begin!

DISNEYLAND

The next day it poured in the morning, but we walked straight into the park and started reminiscing on the main street. Due to Covid, all characters dressed in their Halloween costumes welcomed us from the terrace - this time there was no chance of a hug from Mickey, Pluto or Goofy... Social distancing and masks were compulsory and everybody was in great spirits. The attractions were open and decorated in the spooky style from the Haunted House to the Mississippi paddle boat. The rides have not changed much, and we went on the gentle roller coaster in the Indiana Jones style. Then we walked through the Mexican village celebrating the Day of Death with its numerous skeletons clad in colourful regional outfits surrounded with saguaro cactai - the symbol of the Mexican desert.

We walked through the Sleeping Beauty castle to the Alice in Wonderland maze and the winking Cheshire cat -just like all those years ago ... We went on the spinning cups and the boats meandering round the countries represented by main features and mobile figures in national costumes - it IS a small world after all ... Lunch was near the Star Wars experience: the hamburgers for Emma and me, and the vegan fajitas for Sophie and her partner Mark.

And finally, the youngsters ventured on some stomach-wrenching rollercoaster ride while the birthday girl waited patiently with a cup of coffee wearing the Pluto hat bought 23 years ago – and no longer available...

It was getting dark and we were informed that the traditional daily fireworks were not presented because of Covid (again!), but there would be a display at 9pm to commemorate Guy Fawkes Night. And the display it was... traditionally over Sleeping Beauty's castle...

Memories, memories...

The next day was grey but dry. It was the day I was to present as a Snow White. The challenge was there and I had to comply – shaking and piling layers of tee shirts on my frozen body to emerge as a younger sister of the character. It was a head-turner as the characters were absent from the streets, but I only managed to last for the picture and succumbed to Mother Nature. The change of clothes saved my sanity...

The adjacent park was the Walt Disney Studios, where the various rides through film-themed constructions gave those willing an additional thrill to enjoy. I surrendered and enjoyed the mementoes of the creator of the empire, enormous statues of the characters such as Buzz Lightyear, Mickey Mouse as a conductor in Fantasia and many others. And the whole experience ended in the saloon bar of the hotel with a warming up bourbon and a pleasant chat in great company ... What a birthday time!

PARIS

Next stop was, *Ooh la la Paris!*

My fourth time there: first with my fiancé, then with my parents and the third visit with my brother, his daughter and my girls. We arrived at night and came out of the metro station to face a beautifully lit Opera House. It was founded by Louis XIV in 1669 and located in the spectacular Palais Garnier - his pensive statue guards the building. The hotel was a classic 19th-century building with a winding staircase, a minuscule lift and similar rooms. It prided itself on having given shelter to Oscar Wilde in 1899, who stayed there for a while after overstaying his welcome in more affluent places, which he could not afford. His mementoes adorn the walls with many a saying quoted. The sensational atmosphere in every corner ... bathed in glorious sunshine, with all its famous places of interest uncrowded and open to inquisitive tourists. The best option after walking for miles in Disneyland was the open-top bus - the quickest and laziest way to explore the city of lovers!

Starting with the sights of the gothic Louvre, which is the most visited museum in the world and stores more than a half-a-million works of art, with 35,000 on display. The characteristic glass pyramid welcomes the visitors ready to explore the endless corridors in search of unique treasures, the most attractive being Mona Lisa – the mysterious Joconde ...

Passing by the Place de la Concorde with its 3,300 BC Luxor obelisk and the fountains created to celebrate French commerce and maritime navigation. The place witnessed many executions, including those of royalty during the French Revolution. It is the largest square in the city at the bottom of the Champs Elysees – the avenue leading to the Arc de Triomphe in the Place Charles de Gaulle. It is famous for the theatres, cafes and luxury shops located in the impressive and grandiose buildings, highest prices and lined with elm trees.

From there, we crossed the Seine and admired the panorama on each side of the river. On reaching the Arc, we witnessed the famous traffic jam in which we were stuck 23 years ago and had to circle round the monument six times before we found the lane to get out! It was Napoleon's wish to raise it, but he did not live long enough to appreciate this symbol of victory dedicated to the armies of the Revolution and the Empire.

The Eiffel Tower was towering above, begging us to inspect this wrought iron lattice construction of 132 years, also called the Iron Lady ... It is a global cultural icon of France and the tallest structure in Paris. We got off the bus and enquired regarding a possible trip to the highest observation deck accessible to the public in Europe.

Because of the pandemic, the admission system was very strict, and we were allowed only to walk/catch the lift to level one. However, as I was wearing my 70th birthday badge, an exception was made, and we were allowed to go to the top as my special birthday treat! The views are unforgettable and the memories from decades ago were brought back instantly ... those of my parents, my ex-husband and the daughters when they were young...

The next day we sailed along the river, admiring all the architectural gems, both on land and over the river with endless bridges, and listening to the audio guide telling us the history of this enchanting place. The weather helped and the sights were spectacular - the change of means of transport added to the sightseeing experience. All in the full glory of autumnal sunshine ... clear air ... romantic memories...

Suddenly we passed the Statue of Liberty! Right in the middle of the River Seine on the southern tip of the artificial Isle aux Cygnes! The quarter-scale replica statue was given to the city of Paris by the American community in 1889 to commemorate the centennial of the French Revolution, and to highlight the historically close bond between two nations founded on the republican ideal.

The next stop was at the Louvre Palace - the most visited museum in the world, dating back to medieval times when it served as a fortress. It opened in 1793, and currently, it has more than 500,000 objects of art, with 35,000 on display, from prehistory to the 21st century, including the Mona Lisa and Venus de Milo.

Emma and I walked the endless corridors of this gothic giant, modernized recently with the controversial glass pyramid built to improve the deficiencies of the building and to improve the visitor's access to the museum. We were aiming to find La Giaconda – or help mum relive the encounter from decades ago when visiting Paris for the first time.

Following the mysterious theft in 1911 by an Italian artist and many incidents of vandalism last century, the priceless painting became the centre of security, and nowadays it can be admired only from a distance; the enigmatic smile attracts and mesmerizes the onlookers. The event deserved a family picture, so it was kindly taken by the attendant. Both of us had to hide behind the compulsory masks.

We passed many of the eight departments and were told it would take more than 200 days to see them all! On the way out, we looked at the Venus de Milo towering over the landing in the marble staircase and bid the place goodbye...

And the final day was filled with walking the streets of the City of Love from the hotel to the Opera Garnier House, past Moulin Rouge, all the way up to the architectural gem of gems: the Basilica of Sacre Cour, situated on the Montmartre hill overlooking Paris.

Its byzantine-style construction started in 1870 using local travertine stone and was completed in 1919.

The dome shelters a spectacular mosaic of the risen Christ and many special additions such as a unique organ and a collection of bells. A long staircase leads from the church all the way down to the artists' hub in Montmartre full of famous cafes and restaurants. The artistic atmosphere is nearly palpable with quaint shops, arty posters and small groups enjoying their mid-day coffees...

Walking downwards through impressive edifices and endless restaurants, we reached the Opera House and arrived at our hotel. A quick change of clothes and free time to enjoy the vicinity... spotting the differences and similarities in local habits and tasting local food - so different from the cuisine we are used to in England.

After our return to the Eurostar, of course, we spent a couple of days recovering from the fantastic experience, realizing that the back to reality meant going back to being fully controlled and forced to obey the governmental decisions concerning the never-ending pandemic hysteria. Being exposed to the worrying numbers of infections every day and told of the ever-rising number of deaths by an infamous trio consisting of the chief medic, Prime Minister and one other.

They were pontificating from the pulpits at No10 about the dangers of the virus and the need to save the NHS - a complete misinterpretation of the situation as the NHS was established to save us ... That is on top of strongly advised vaccinations – produced and approved over a very short period of time, which raised public concerns as to their efficacy and safety. Not forgetting the lateral tests and other versions of testing of questionable accuracy. And the compulsory masks in public places ...

After two years of this experimental attempt to control the virus, it became clear that we have to learn to live with it - as with millions of other microbes that emerged in human history - and after much deliberation and consultation, common sense prevailed, and all the restrictions have been abandoned!

So, we can continue to enjoy the travels and learning about other tribes, cultures, environments and nature's innumerable secrets, or at least hoping to do so, to make our dreams come true. Positive thinking will prevail in spite of the current political and military developments. The West and the East divide has been resurrected in a new Cold War - as it was 60 years ago - and this time leading to a senseless, brutal and frightening reality of relentless destruction of human lives, homes and spirits.

True war refugees scattering all over Central Europe and further afield, hoping to return to their homeland one day. But the prospects are grim ... and the fear of a first nuclear conflict in the world is spreading and does not help the general mood.

Poland is proving to be expertly organised in helping the misplaced families gathering at its eastern border, with more than half a million being allowed to enter my country and find a safe shelter for mainly mothers and children in the private homes of the Poles. The humanitarian action is perfectly organised, with the taxis pulling up at the rest centres and taking - free of charge - the needy displaced to secure, warm and welcoming homes - away from the "heroics" of war...

There are also deliveries to the attacked neighbour supplying food, clothes, and even petrol as the whole infrastructure has been damaged, both by the occupant and the subversive moves of the national army blowing up the bridges and the roads to slow down the advance of the aggressor. And the worst fears are about the takeover of Europe's biggest nuclear plant - the promise of worse things to come from the power-thirsty leader of the bullies still is ringing in our ears! And the world is watching and following the advances in anticipation...

So, hope is the only solution: that humans will communicate effectively to resolve the conflict and that positive human traits will win over greed and irrationality. As in the recent past, history runs in circles, but to the tragic effect of five years of hideous crimes and indescribable suffering on every level of human existence.

And interestingly, there has not been a single day without war since then on our unique planet – how destructive we are! And how little attention is paid to our environment... Most solutions for protecting it and restoring it have failed and the pollution levels of every kind have never been higher.

We live in critical times of insecurity, uncertainty and cataclysms – the pay- back time for our arrogance and ignorance in not taking Mother Nature seriously. And the time to recover is narrowing zero. That, in addition to what the Universe is preparing to serve on us...

Positive thoughts create positive things, and things should get better with time...

And remember: smiles are contagious and kindness is free...

www.ingramcontent.com/pod-product-compliance
Lightning Source LLC
Chambersburg PA
CBHW040844120626
46547CB00001B/14